THE BOOK OF
MORCHARD BISHOP

THE BOOK OF
MORCHARD BISHOP

A DEVONSHIRE HEARTLAND PARISH

COMPILED AND EDITED BY JEFF KINGABY

HALSGROVE

First published in Great Britain in 1999

Copyright © 1999 JEFF KINGABY

All rights reserved. No part of this publication may be reproduced, stored in a retrieval system, or transmitted in any form or by any means without the prior permission of the copyright holder.

British Library Cataloguing-in-Publication Data
A CIP record for this title is available from the British Library

ISBN 1 84114 037 6

HALSGROVE
PUBLISHING, MEDIA AND DISTRIBUTION

Halsgrove House
Lower Moor Way
Tiverton, Devon EX16 6SS
Tel: 01884 243242
Fax: 01884 243325
http://www.halsgrove.com

Printed and bound in Great Britain by Bookcraft Ltd., Midsomer Norton

DEDICATION

This book is dedicated to the people of Morchard Bishop Parish, past and present.

Morchard Thatch, sketch by Julie Rudge

Foreword

Most readers will appreciate that a great deal of research has gone into this book; interviewing local residents, perusing newspaper records, parish council and school records, sorting out old newspaper cuttings, maps, documents, photographs and other sources. Many people would ask 'But where do you start?' The answer was simple – Marion Mills.

Everybody in the parish knows that Marion is the unofficial parish historian. She has a vast knowledge of local history, and perhaps because she lives in the oldest house in the parish (14th century Rudge), she has been inspired to collect many photos, cuttings, documents and maps over the years.

In the 1980s when Tim Lyddon produced the excellent audio-visual presentation, 'The Making of Morchard', he obtained much of his information, photos and documents from Marion's collection. In 1981 she was the driving force behind the two-day exhibition 'The Morchard Memories', held in the Memorial Hall (see chapter 5). For many years she has been a leading light in the Chulmleigh and District History Society. Our thanks are also due to her for researching two of the chapters in this book, 'Farming' and 'The Church and Chapels'. In the latter chapter another member of the History Society, Ruth Stanton, also assisted her in her task.

Richard Knight is another member of the history society and our thanks are due to him for not only researching the chapter on 'Occupations, Trade and Commerce' but for the large number of photographs which he has taken over the last year, which appear in this publication.

The chapters on 'Home Life' and 'Transport and Communications' were difficult subjects to research but Julie Page did an excellent job. She was responsible for discovering the 1905 article 'A visit to Morchard Bishop' in the Devon Record Office, which helps to give a very clear picture of life in the village during the early part of the century. In the past Julie has played a major part in various village activities, including helping to produce the *Village Appraisal*, acting as a founder member of the Recycling Group and helping with the production of the famous *Morchard Bishop Cook Book*.

Thanks also to Julie Rudge, another person who had given so much to the parish, for her excellent sketches, which really illustrated something that other pictures cannot portray. How else could one depict the 'Skimmity Ride'?

We are grateful to Jacqueline Patten for researching part of 'School Days' and to Nannette Brown for her help with 'Entertainment and Leisure'. Also to the many people who have supplied us with information about their clubs and organisations; in many cases they went to a lot of trouble to trace old photographs and documents.

Although we have been able to confirm much of the information in this book, in some cases we have had to rely on individuals' memories without corroboration and, as we all know, time does strange things to one's memory – in all cases we have, however, tried our hardest to be accurate.

Jeff Kingaby

Contents

Foreword — 6
Acknowledgements — 9
Introduction — 11
Kelly's Directory for 1902 and 1939 — 12

1 Early History — 15
2 The Parish Council — 19
3 The Church and Chapels — 25
4 School Days — 33
5 Entertainment and Leisure — 43
6 Transport and Communications — 63
7 Farming — 69
8 Home Life — 89
9 Occupations, Trade and Commerce — 101
10 Serving the Parish — 109
11 The War Years — 121
12 Sport and Recreation — 131
13 A Morchard Miscellany — 141

List of Subscribers — 157

Acknowledgements

Following the successful Morchard Bishop Souvenir Programme for VE Day in 1995, our book group agreed to write this volume for the millennium. Others later joined us and gradually, after several setbacks, we finally made it. Having said that, this book would not have been possible without the help, enthusiasm and support given by the parishioners of Morchard Bishop – those of today and yesterday. A special thanks must be given to all those who have lent photographs and memorabilia, and remembered how things were years ago:

Sonja Andrews, Doris and Joe Burrow, Bert Brimilcombe, Mary and Phil Bourne, Bill Brown, Janice and Terry Butler, Ray Burrow, Aithna Brooks, Maureen Carr, Steve and Roger Carter, John Child, Marina Down, Pam Macey, Gordon and Margaret Dockings, Aubrey Edwards, Diana Farrant, Gill Gunn, David Gribble, Sheila Gurl, Vera Gillbard, Jackie Galton, Susan Gales, Freda and Mervyn Heggadon, Roger Holloway, Chris and Caril Hutchings, Anne and Stephen Hargreaves, Edwin Hutchings, Sonia Heath, Louie and Brenda James, Diana Johnson, Anne and Howard Jones, the staff of Morchard Bishop School, Terry Nott, Alison and Tony Kilburn, Graham Lewis, Ida and John Lucas, Tim Lyddon, George Matthews, Jane Magor, Florence Milden, Mary North, Ann Palmer, Hilda and Keith Partrige, Bob Pope, Dawn and Charles Parkhouse, J. Pugsley, Pam Pickard, Roger Quick, Julie Rudge, Les Rice, Geoff Rice, Yvonne and Norman Rice, Jackie Rowcliffe, Mary Richards, Mervyn Rice, Marion Rice, Rev. Brian Shillingford, Janet Symons, Jo Savage, Mark Stevens, Henry and Dora Tucker, Mike and Mary Tyler, Teresa Tyldesley, Ruth Taylor, Sandra, Hilda and Maurice Wedlake, Harold and Mervyn Webber, Penny Whicher and F. J. Michael and Elsie Yendall.

Our thanks also to the help and assistance given by the following:

Crediton Courier, Express and Echo, Mark Stephen's book, *Ernest Bevin, The North Devon Journal* and Roger Gimley's recent publication, *Wheels Around Witheridge*.

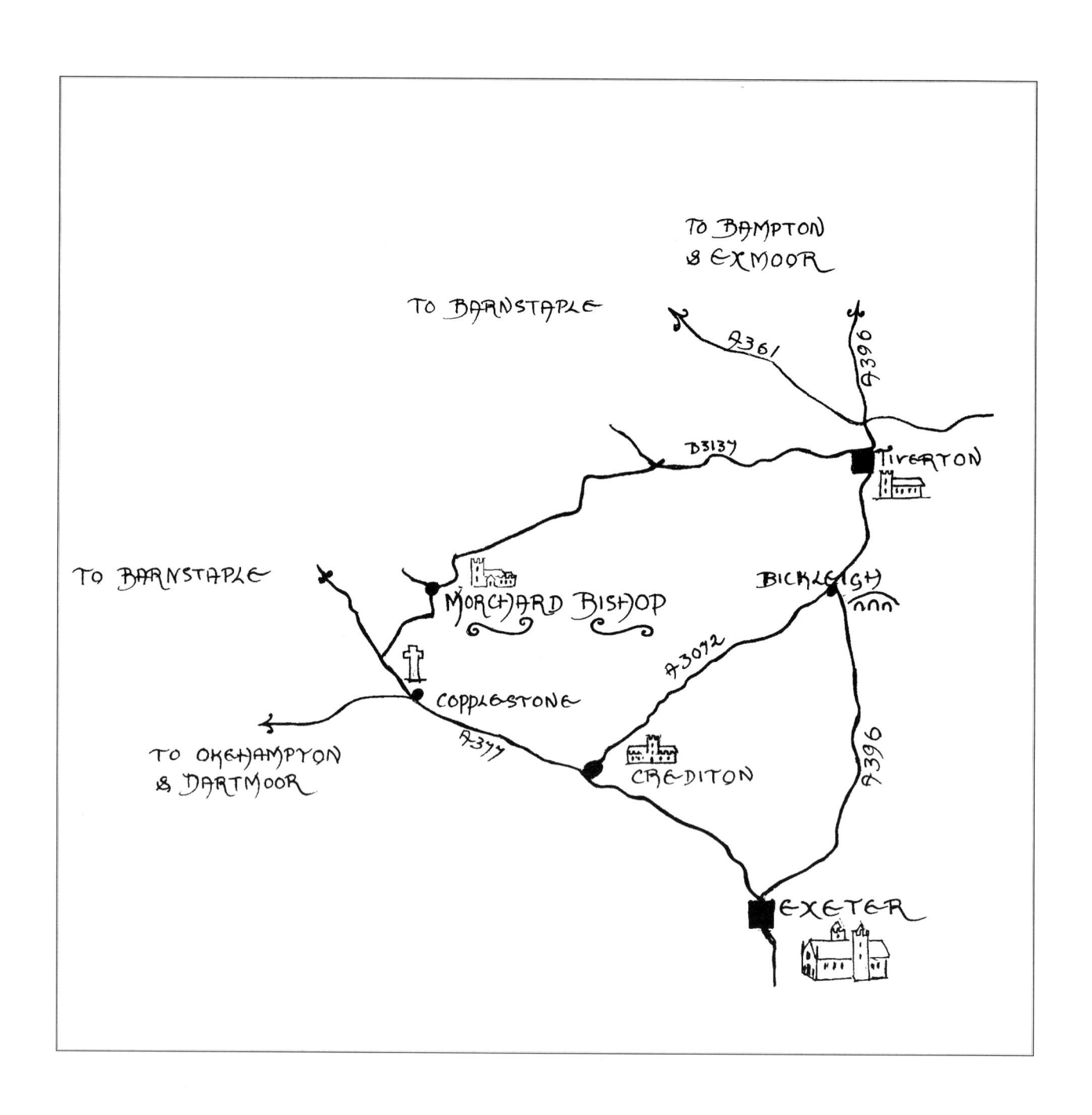

Introduction

Morchard Bishop nestles comfortably in the very heartland of Devon, midway between the north and south coast and sitting between the two great moors, Dartmoor and Exmoor. This is hilly, unspoilt countryside, with magnificent views around every bend of our narrow lanes, yet within reasonable travelling distance of Crediton, Tiverton and the City of Exeter, with its cathedral and university. It is one of the largest parishes in the county, with a population of just under 1000 and a mixture of all age groups.

The village overlooks hundreds of small fields bordered by a network of ancient Devon banks that have mercifully escaped the bulldozer and the fate of arable farmland in eastern England. These banks have traditionally suited the dairy, beef and sheep industry that, despite having been modernised over the last 50 years, still retains many ancient cob, stone and thatched buildings. The parish is proud that it has the longest row of terraced thatched cottages in England, and many buildings that were built in the 14th and 15th centuries. In the 1980s, parishioners voted overwhelmingly for it to become a conservation area.

However, Morchard Bishop has not escaped times of adversity. Once on the stage route from Barnstaple to London it saw the building of the turnpike road in the 1830s and later the railway line – both ignored the village. Both the wool trade, which moved to the North of England, and the Honiton Lace Industry, became mechanised. All this had an adverse affect on an area that had been so very prosperous in the 1830s. To add further to the problems, agriculture declined and gradually rural depopulation increased as talented young men like John and Samuel Way boarded ships in Plymouth to make a new life in Australia and New Zealand. Similarly, young leaders like Ernest Bevin deserted the land and sought a brighter future in Bristol and other large cities.

Because the parish had lost half its population over a 30-year period, the *Gazette* newspaper commissioned a reporter to visit the area and establish why the rural depopulation was worse in Morchard than in adjoining areas. The poverty and poor living conditions, coupled with bad housing, were so very obvious but the inhabitants still retained their sense of pride and community spirit. Perhaps it was this great poverty in a community that had little contact with the outside world which made them such a caring society, helping one another until they could no longer manage and then deserting for the cities in their scores.

The Second World War made an big impact. Farming incomes improved the local economy and parishioners saw many changes; the conscription of their young folk, the arrival of service personnel, Land Army girls, and even prisoners of war, moved into their isolated parish. They cared for a large number of evacuees from the blitz cities who sought shelter here and they made them very welcome.

Over the next three decades the standard of living improved, mobility increased, townsfolk moved down into the area in search of a tranquil setting and the population began to rise again.

Once again the parishioners were prepared to welcome 'outsiders' into their village. The 'outsiders' children grew up alongside the locals, and many in turn have settled in the area. One only has to read this book to realise that this is a very happy, friendly village - a fact which was confirmed a few years ago in the *Village Appraisal* – no wonder the local estate agents call it a 'sociable village'. I, as an outsider of 21 years (perhaps a local now!), love this parish and feel very proud to have been able to help compile this book. Thank you.

Finally, may I thank the other members of the Morchard Bishop Book Group for their encouragement, hard work and loyalty, and my wife Molly, who has been ever-patient with me.

Jeff Kingaby,
West Aish,
Morchard Bishop,
e-mail: su2195@eclipse.co.uk
May 1999

Kelly's Directory 1902

Morchard Bishop is a large parish and village on the old road from Exeter to Barnstaple, 2 miles north east from Morchard Road station on the north Devon branch of the London and South Western Railway.

The church of St Mary is an ancient building of stone in the Perpendicular style, consisting of chancel, nave, aisles, south porch, and an embattled western tower with pinnacles containing 6 bells: in the south aisle are two mutilated recumbent effigies in freestone of a civilian and wife of the 16th century, assumed to represent Sir John Eyston, of Eyston, or Easton in this parish, and Margaret (Arundel) his wife, there is also a monument, with arms, to Gabriel Greene gent ob. Nov 2, 1685, and Dorothy his wife, ob. 10 April, 1660 and some remains of oak screens also exist: the church was restored in 1889 at a cost of £1,928, and now affords 260 sittings. The register dates from the year 1660. The living is a rectory, net yearly value £654, including 178 acres of glebe, with residence, in the gift of Mrs. R. Bartholomew, and held since 1898 by the Rev. Herbert Springett Watkins B.A. of Durham University. Here are Congregational and Bible Christian chapels. There are charities of £60 yearly value; in addition one of £10 a year, left in 1733 by Mrs. Thomasine Tucker, for the education and clothing of eight girls and boys. A small charity payable out of the Rudge estate was revived in 1887 by William Henry Kelland esq. as a memorial to his mother, the maternal granddaughter of the late P. Kelland, of Rudge and Bowerthy in Lapford.

A fair is held on the first Monday after the 9th September, yearly, for cattle. Beech Hill, the residence of Charles Comyns Tucker esq. J.P. is a pleasant mansion, originally built c. 1707, during the reign of Queen Anne; it was restored in 1810; and almost entirely rebuilt in 1817. Barton House, half a mile north-east, a handsome modern residence, is the residence of the Hon. John Fellowes Wallop. Aish House, the property of C. Mortimer esq. is at present unoccupied. The rector is lord of the manor. The Hon. John F. Wallop, who is lord of Barton Manor, Charles Comyn Tucker esq. J.P. William Tucker Arundel Radford, of Nymet Rowland, Frank Saunders and Charles Mortimer esqrs. and the Messrs. Leach the chief landowners. The soil is loam and clay, and the sub-soil is clay and shale. The chief crops are wheat and barley. The area is 7,169 acres; rateable value, £6,728 the population in 1901 was 985.

Parish Clerk, Thomas Zeal. Post, M.O. & T.O., T.M.O., S.B., Express Delivery Parcel & Annuity & Insurance Office (Railway Sub Office. Letters should have R.S.O. North Devon added). – Miss Louisa Catherine Tolley, subpostmistress. Letters dispatched 5 & 10.15 am. & 8.15 pm Sunday, 8.15 p m; deliveries 7 a.m. & 3.45pm: Sunday, 7 a.m. Wall Letter Box at Oldboro', cleared at 7p.m.

Church Schools (mixed & infants), erected in 1872, for 250 children, average attendance, 65 boys, 56 girls & 41 infants. Thomas Zeal, master; Mrs. Catherine Zeal mistress

Carriers to Exeter - Jn Coneybeer & Mathew Wreford, on Fri. returning same day; to Railway station, Morchard Road, Frederick Howe

Morchard Road Railway station, Wm. Lovell, stationmaster.

Allen Humphrey, Alma cottage
Brown Misses, Woodgate
Morris Mrs, White's Cottage
Tucker Chas. Cowyns JP Beech Hill
Wallop Hon. John. Fellowes, Barton ho
Watkins Rev. Herbert Springett B.A. Rectory

COMMERCIAL,

Allen Humphrey M.R.C.S. Eng., L.R.C.P. Lond. surgeon & medical officer & public vaccinator for Morchard Bishop district, Crediton union, Alma cottage.
Bennett Albert Webber, The Fountain P.R
Bennett Alfred, shopkeeper
Bennett Thomas Arthur, - Farmer: Wood Barton
Bowden -, farmer, East Middle Leigh
Brownson John, boot maker
Burrow George, tailor
Burrow Jane (Mrs.), London Inn
Caun George, farmer, Knightstone
Coneybeer Henry, baker
Coneybeer Robert, farmer & carrier
Coneybeer Thomas, saddler
Cousins George, farmer, Oxon park
Drew Bros. engineers & machinists
Drew Rbt. agricultural implement ma.
Drew William, carpenter
Elston Anna (Miss), point lace maker
Elworthy Hugh, butcher
Ford Geo. draper & grocer,The Green
Friend Frederick, farmer, Mare
Grant Robert Tucker, farmer & Butcher landowner, Old Borough
Hammacott William, farmer & miller (water) Wigham
Harris John farmer Week Barton
Haydon George farmer
Heard Hy. dairyman Highr. Middlecott
Howard Frank farmer Paradise
Howe Frederick, carrier to the Station, Church street
James Frank thatcher
Kelland Wm. Hy. farmer, Middlecott
Kingdom Charles, Rudge Rew
Kingdon Frederick Comyns, yeoman, Upcott.
Leach Frederick, farmer, Ingodown
Leach John, farmer East Ash
Leach William, assitant overseer, Frost
Leach William, farmer & landowner, Middle Week
Leach Henry, yeoman, Southcott
Lewis Wm. dairyman, Lower Week
Madge William, farmer, Shores
Mallett Edwin F. relieving officer & registrar of births, deaths & marriages for Morchard Bishop district of Crediton union.
More Grace (Miss), berlin wool dealer
Mears, George, farmer, Moore
Mortimer Charles, yeoman, Broadgate
Mortimore Albert, nurseryman, Harinolls
Olding John, farmer, Tatepath
Pack William, farmer, Brownstone
Passmore, Samuel timber haulier & road contractor, Frost.
Phillips Fred, farmer, Brownstone
Phillips John grocer draper, ironmonger, seedsman & general supply stores agent for J F Mortimer & Co dyers, & Cleaners
Pope John, farmer Crockers
Pugsley Mark watch & deck maker
Pugsley Mary Jane (Mrs), grocer
Reed William, draper
Rice Francis builder & agricultural implement maker
Rice George agricultural implement maker, Frost
Rodd John, farmer, Rolestone Barton
Saunder Frank, Yeoman Rudge Barton
Shobbrook Jn. farmer, Chillingford
Smith Thomas & Charles, blacksmiths
Southcott William, tailor
Star John, builder, wheelwright & English timber merchant
Stoneman Richard, miller (water) Bugford mill
Tucker Emma (Miss), frmr. landland
Tucker Henry, farmer, Stone ash.
Tucker John, farmer, Bishopleigh
Tucker Robert, farmer, Leigh
Tucker Samuel, farmer, Lower Venn
Tucker Thomas, yeoman Leigh
Tucker Thomas, yeoman Slade.
Tucker Waker farmer North wood.
Warren Thomas, farmer, Hill
Way James, baker & boot maker
Webber Arundel, blacksmith
Webber Wm. farmer. Easton Barton
Wreford John, grocer

Kelly's Directory 1939

MORCHARD BISHOP
Comments additional to those made in the 1902 Directory.

Electricity is available. Water is supplied by Crediton Rural District Council. The ancient oak screen was restored to the church in 1930. The population in 1931 was 829.

COMMERCIAL SECTION

Marked thus * farm 150 acres or over.

Bennett Alfd. farmer
* Bennett Arth. Fredk. farmer, Week Barton & Ridgeway
Bennett Bessie (Mrs.), shopkpr. Church St
Bowden Wltr. farmer, Higher Venn
Brewer Arch. farmer, Quicks' Tenement
Brewer Ja. carpntr. Higher Old Borough
* Brewer Tn. farmer, Moore
Brewer Wm. farmr. Low. Old Borough
Buckingham Alpha, farmer, Higher Middlecott
Burrow Eros. tailors, & post office. TN 25
Cann Rt. boot & shoe repr. Chapel St.
Chanter Jn. bldr. The Green
Chapple Thos. farmer, Wigham
Colton Jasper Thos. farmer, Stone Ash
Cousins Fras. farmer, Oxon pk
*Daymond Stanley, farmer, Rolestone Barton
Devon County Council, quarry renters Bugford. Lapford 21
Diamond Fras. Claude Elliott L.M.S.S.A. Lond. physcn. & surgn. Grebertrees. TN26
Dockings Harry, farmer,. East Sharland. Copplestone 219
* Dockings Percy, farmer, Southcott & Dinnicombe. Copplestone 210
Down Japh. shopkpr. Fore St
*Down Sidney Thos. yeoman, Rudge
Drew Bros. engnrs. TN 29
Drew Albt. boot & shoe mkr. 5 Fore st
Drew Edwin, bldr. Fore St
Edworthy Regid. & Wm. small holders, New ho.
Elworthy Thos. Hy. farmer, Middle Weeke.
Ex-Service Men's Club (P. Andrews sec.), Memorial hall
Ford Jas. tailor, Trelawney
Ford Reginald G. W. draper, grocer & boot & shoe dealer, The Green
Frost Fanny (Miss), shopkpr
Frost Wm. thatcher, Chapel St
Fry Thos. smallholder, Brownstone

Greenslade Thos. farmer, Lane End
Gunn Ernest William, wholesale butcher, Woolsgrove (letters through Copplestone). T N Copplestone 226
Hammett Benj. farmer, Middle Ash
Harris Thos Oco. & M. A. (Miss) smallholders, Ivy cott
Hayden Rt. Geo. farmer, Watcombe
Haydon Wm. farmer, Woodgate
Hill Jn. Bucknell, farmer, Higher Brownstone
Holland Wm. farmer, Middleleigh
Hooper Frank, farmer, Knightstone Down
Howard Herbt. farmer, Venn Farm. T N 23
* Hutchings Cecil Frank, farmer, Middlecott
Hutchings Edwin Maurice, farmer, Easton Barton (letters through Copplestone). Lapford 34
Isaac A. farmer, Scotland
Lavelle Anthony Fras. dentist (attends mon. 5 to 6p.m.), Church St
London Inn (Chas. Hilliard). TN22
* Maunder Hy. farmer, Knathorne
Melhuish Albt. farmer, Ingodown
Memorial Hall (The Earl of Portsmouth, D. Tipper esq. & the National Council of Social Service trustees)
Milton Chas. farmer, Bonds Middlecott
* Mortimer Chas. farmer, Aish
National Provincial Bank Ltd (agency to Crediton) (Basil Hy Applebee Eames, manager) (open tues & thurs. & fair days 10 a.m to 12.30 p.m.); head office, 15 Bishopsgate, London E C 2
Oatway Thos farmer, Chillingford TN39
*Oatway Thos. jun. farmer, Hill TN41
Otton Maurice, butcher, Fairfield TN32
Pack Wm. farmer, Paradise
Palfrey Florence Mary (Miss) draper, Church St
Palfrey Stafford Llewllyn, farmer, Old Borough
Partridge Archbld. Edwd. smallholder, The Laurels
Partridge Jn. farmer, Broadridge
Palfrey Florence Mary (Miss),
Petherick Archbld. farmr. The Parks
Phillips Alfd. insur. agt. Steps cott
Phillips Winifred (Miss), grocer & draper
Pope Hilda (Miss), district nurse
Pugsley Wm. farmer, Mare
Pulsford Chas. smallholder, Shores Farm
Raymont Wm. baker, The Bakery, Fore St
Rice Sydney & Alfd. Ernest, butchrs
Rice William, yeoman, Crookstock
Richards Albt. Saml. farmer, Tate path & Hartscombe
Roberts Alfd. farmer, Farthing pk
* Rogers Wm. Bartholomew Baker, farmer, Broadgate
* Saunders Bernard, farmer, East Aish
Shapland Fras. Jn. yeoman, Shobrooke (letters through Copplestone) Copplestone 253

Skinner Lewis Jn. fruit grower, Hartnolls T N 30
* Slade Saml. farmer, Rudge Rew
Smith Chas. A.F.C.L. blacksmith
Snell Clifford Aubrey, motor engineer & cycle dealer; accumulator service station, London Inn garage T N 22
Stoneman Rd. dog breeder, Bugford. Lapford 37
Symes Wm. Lionel, grocer, Fountain head
* Tucker Albt. Jas. farmer, Slade
Tucker Geo. farmer, North Leigh
Tucker Hedley Jn. frmr. Langland
* Tucker Jn. farmer; Upcott
Webber Brothers, blacksmiths, Frost
* Wedlake Thos. farmer, Brownstone
William Albert Leslie, baker & pastrycook, Steam Bakery. T N 33
Wills Jsph. farmer, The Elms
Wood Walter, farmer, North Wood
Woodman Wm. farmer, Hayland
* Yendell Fredk. farmer, Wood Barton. TN34

Centre of the village on the Tithe Map of 1840

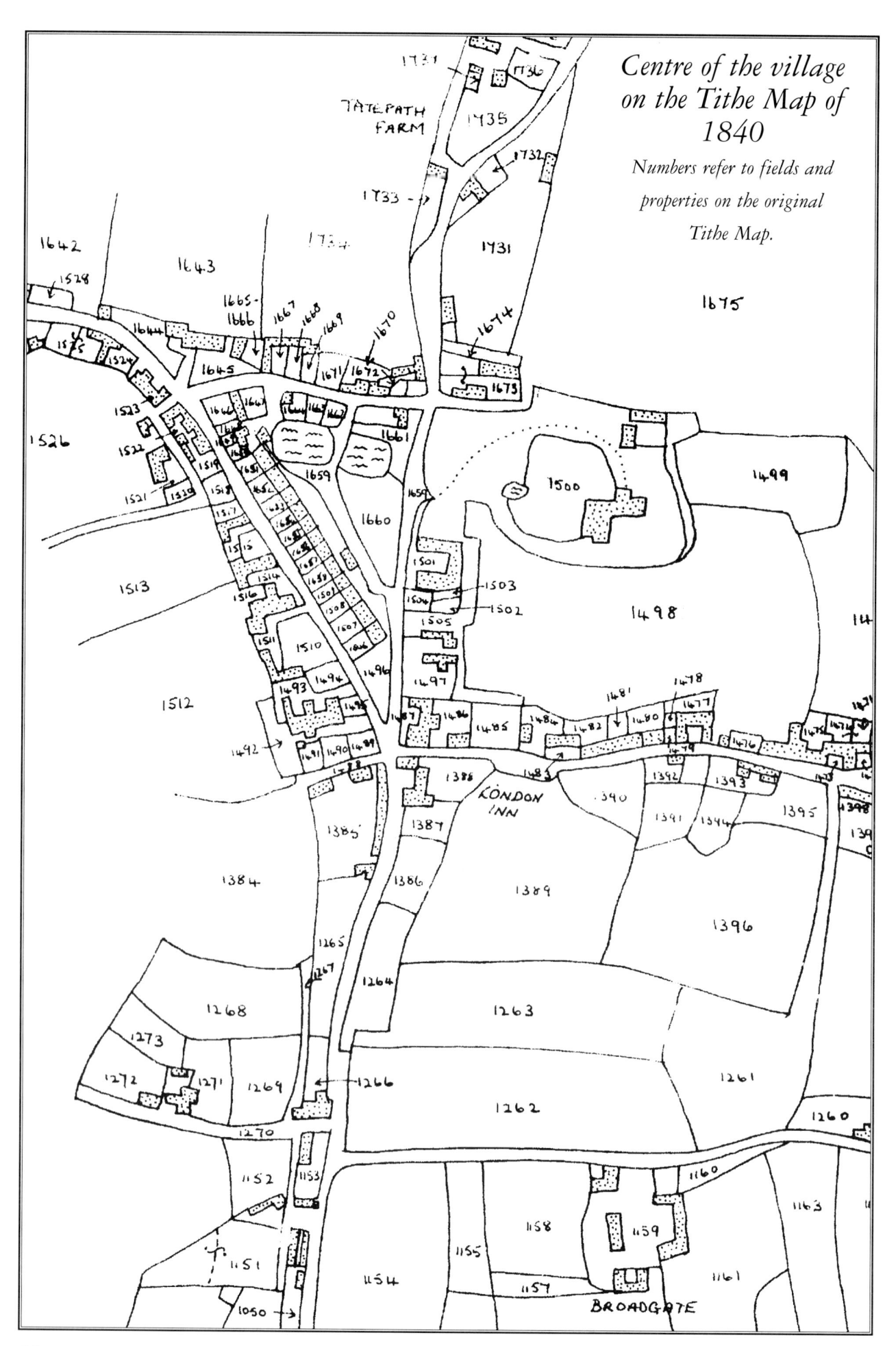

Numbers refer to fields and properties on the original Tithe Map.

Chapter 1: Early History

The history of Morchard Bishop can be traced back to Celtic times when it was called Morchet. The name originated from two celtic words, 'mor' meaning big or great, and 'coed' meaning wood. The settlement was in or near a great wood. The site of the encampment was probably in the Orchardy – the field next to the church where there is a pond with a never-failing water supply. The surrounding land would have been a wilderness of trees, undergrowth and high, open moorland, and the valleys would have had marshy bottoms

The Celts would have lived in roundhouses and have kept chickens, Dexter cows and Soay sheep. The pitch of the rafters had to be 45 degrees or the thatch would have leaked, and this was the reason for the building having its distinctive 'witch's hat' look. There being no hole in the roof from which the smoke could escape, it trickled out through the thatch killing off creepy-crawlies and curing any food hung up in the roof space. The Celts would have used a bread oven to cook their dough that they made from flour ground in a quern. Their tartan clothes would have been woven on a loom.

Morchet was on the Celtic Way, a vast communication system which cut across our area from Witheridge to Winkleigh. The track stuck to the safer hill-tops as much as possible, only descending into the dangerous valleys to cross the streams.

From Witheridge the way forded the river Dalch, a celtic word meaning 'dark water', and continued through to Washford Pine, Black Dog and Berry Castle, where it met another path coming from Hele Lane and Thelbridge Cross. From Berry Castle the way went through West Emletts and East Emletts, from where the path forded a stream and then went along the 'Sunk Way' to the farm called Scotland to meet a track from Kennerleigh. From Scotland the track passed Hare Street (a Saxon name), on its way to Moor Farm, Butcombe Lane, Merchants Corner and then Broadgates leading on to the church at Orchardy.

The path then went down Church Street, past the old Congregational Chapel and across the fields. Although there is no track there any longer, the alignment of all the gates denotes the original route. The path then passes Middlecott on its way to Bugford, Nymet Rowland and Winkleigh.

The Celts then had an elaborate network of communication and a pond on the top of a hill was a useful stop-over on a journey. This was the making of Morchard.

The only known Celtic site in the area is at Rudge, where, between 1985-89, Professor Todd and his students from Exeter University carried out a dig. Excavations revealed that there was a site enclosed by a ditch on a hill, with extensive look-outs to the south and west and an excellent water supply nearby. The inside area, which measured about 90 by 40 feet, was metalled and had storage pits, some containing pottery dating back to c.AD50. A number of post holes were found, probably for the posts which held up the wall of a roundhouse, which must have been around 30 feet in diameter.

In 661, the Saxons under King Cenwalh attacked the Celts at the hill fort at Posbury. The Saxons won and took over the surrounding areas, including Morchard Bishop.

The Anglo-Saxons disregarded the natives, at least in the early days, and did not mix with them. It is probable that they founded their settlement to the north of the ridge where the main part of the village still is, and set aside the land to the south and east for agriculture. The cottages on the east side of Fore Street were not built until the 18th century and without these the village would have taken on the usual Anglo-Saxon square shape, albeit truncated at the top. They got their water from two large ponds at the bottom of the village. They were still there until early this century, but now form part of a garden.

Under the Anglo-Saxons it was the duty of the citizens themselves to see that the laws were not broken. They were organised into groups of ten families called 'tythings'. Each member of the tything was responsible for the good behaviour of the others. If somebody committed a crime the others had to bring him to the court or 'moot'. More serious cases went to the 'hundred court' headed by a 'reeve', or the 'shire court' headed by a 'shire reeve' (the origin of our word sheriff).

Before the Norman Conquest the Manor of Morchat belonged to Brictric, Thane of Gloucester and son of Algar, a Saxon nobleman. Britric was sent by King Edward the Confessor to act as ambassador to the Baldwin Court of Flanders. While there he was noticed by Baldwin's daughter Matilda, who fell in love with him and wanted to marry him. The feeling was not mutual however, and later she married William of Normandy.

After Edward died in January 1066, Harold, his brother-in-law, claimed the throne – and so too did Edward's cousin, William of Normandy. Their two armies fought a battle at Hastings, Harold was killed and William became King.

Matilda, now Queen of England, decided to wreak her revenge on Britric and persuaded her husband to seize his lands. Britric was taken to Winchester Castle and there he died. His lands were given to Matilda and on her death in 1083 they reverted to the King.

King William sent out commissioners to make an accurate record of the conquered land and its people. The Domesday Book, as it was called, was completed in 1086. In it we find that Morchet Morcesta was split into at least three separate manors; one belonging to Britric himself, a second being at Shepbrook (probably the present-day Shobrook Farm), and a third comprising the southern part which included Rudge, Southcott and Rolestone Barton and belonged to the manor of Crediton.

Town Barton or Town Farm, the home of the lord of the manor, was at the northern end of the present churchyard and was still there on the tythe map of 1838. A little later it was pulled down and rebuilt as the present Wood Barton.

In 1166 Henry II sold Morchet to the Bishop of Exeter. The See was transferred from Crediton to Exeter in 1050. The price the Bishop paid was 100 marcs or, in today's money, £40. By the start of the 13th century the area was known as Morchet Episcopi and by the 14th century, Bishop's Morchard.

In the Bishop's records of 1387 we read of deer-stealing in Morchard Park. This seems to have been a perpetual problem for it was still being recorded in 1439. We read that in 1451 Bishop Lacey granted 'A 40 day indulgence to all sincere people so that they shall contribute a part of the substance which God has blessed them' – this was to raise money for building a new church. The first rector was Nicholas, the Bishop's Chamberlain, and he was instituted on 22 May 1258.

It is likely that Christianity came to Morchet before the Anglo-Saxons, as most of the area had been christianised by priests from Ireland, Brittany and Cornwall. It is quite possible that the site of the present church was also the site of a Celtic wooden cross where early Christians met, to be superceded by a stone cross, then a wooden building and, finally, today's church, built in 1451. Gabriel Green, a member of the Eyston family, who died in 1485, was reeve for monastic properties and paid for the south aisle.

The rood screen was built in 1490, removed in the 17th century, made into a tower screen in 1840, and finally restored as a rood screen in the 1930s. Morchard Bishop remained the property of the Bishop of Exeter until 1548 when Bishop Vesey was forced by the policies of King Henry VIII to sell it.

The land was 'enclosed', probably in the 14th and 15th centuries, creating many small farms (mainly dairy) and several hamlets. This led to a class of landless labourers dependent on wages.

In 1569 home defence units were set up ready to combat the threat of invasion by the Spanish Armada. John Easton and John Rudge presented the Morchard Bishop section of the Devon muster roll; they reported that they had 16 archers, 10 harquebusiers, 10 pike men and 10 billmen. Fire beacons were built ready to convey news of an invasion and each spot was chosen not only for a local warning but also as part of a chain. The nearest one to Morchard was at Beacon Cross near New Buildings, linking Crediton with Chawleigh.

At the outbreak of the Civil War in 1642 Devon largely supported the Parliamentarians and Cornwall the Royalists, but by 1643 all of Devon except Plymouth was in the King's hands. In February 1644 Devonians had to take an oath of loyalty to the King, any one who refused being subject to imprisonment. Meanwhile the Parliamentarians had developed a well-disciplined, well-trained army under one commander, Sir Thomas Fairfax. They crossed the Devon border, laid seige to Exeter and then moved on to Crediton, where Fairfax learned that the King was marching south to Exeter and that Lord Hopton was approaching from Cornwall. Realising that if he didn't get to Barnstaple soon he might get trapped between the two armies, Fairfax promptly left his heavy baggage at Crediton and marched north. (The rush was such that Cromwell left a pair of boots there and another officer forgot his coat.) Fairfax took with him five regiments of foot, five troops of dragoons and a further five regiments of horse under the command of Oliver Cromwell. Later that day, Saturday 14 February 1646, they marched in the rain through Morchard Bishop and on to Chulmleigh.

On the Monday the Roundheads headed for Torrington where the Royalists were making a stand. This was a good place to defend, as it could only be attacked from the east. By five o'clock that evening Fairfax was about a mile from the town and made camp at Stevenstone House. In those days actions were fought only by day, but the battle of Torrington was to prove a different story.

At midnight Cromwell sent out scouts. Later he thought that they were being attacked and so sent up reinforcements. His well-disciplined troops stuck together in the dark. The Roundheads captured the parish church and used it as a place to keep their prisoners but what they did not know was that it was the Royalist's ammunition dump and contained 80 barrels of gunpowder – the explosion was sudden and unexpected. All inside were killed, the church was completely destroyed and so great were the pyrotechnics that the remaining Royalists fled and the town was taken. The event went down in history as being the first military night action.

Morchard had become relatively prosperous by the beginning of the 19th century. The village was largely self-contained and had generated all the necessary tradesmen required for its well-being. Records of population figures go back to 1750 when there were 1425 people living in the village. This increased to a peak of 1854 in 1851 and then slumped to 780 in 1961. The 1971 figures showed an upturn to 865. The population probably slumped after 1851 with the end of the woollen trade and the building of the valley road.

In 1750 an average of 8.9 people lived in each house. By 1971, this had dropped to only 2.7. It is interesting to note that, if this trend continues, by the year 3000 everyone will be living alone!

Morchard has one of the most complete sets of parish registers in Devon, dating back to 1660, although a few families such as the Eastons, Rudges and Shobrookes can even be traced from the 1332 subsidy rolls. Among the earliest entries are the families of Rice, Cann, Tucker and Webber, members of which are in the village today.

There are several old farmhouses, the oldest being Rudge built in 1320, and Middle Aish (c.1400). Beech Hill (home to the Comyns family) was rebuilt in 1896 and Barton House was built in 1830 by the Churchill family and stayed in their ownership until Lord Portsmouth sold it in 1939.

The 18th century saw the building of the memorial in Morchard Woods to Peter Comyns of Beech Hill which reads:

To the memory of Peter Comyns, Esq. The late worthy proprietor of these rural scenes. He lived beloved and esteemed. A truly virtuous man, and died lamented. A sincere and exemplary Christian. Go thou and do likewise. Erected MDCCLXX (1770).

In 1762, eight years earlier, the church had a double-deck pulpit built. It cost 16 guineas and was not removed until 1951 when the woodworm finally won. The Rectory was built in 1790. It had 26 rooms including 11 bedrooms, and 3 staircases. It, too, survived until the 1950s and then fell into decay and was sold for development. The present bungalow estate of Old Rectory Gardens was built on the site.

The village has two links with Napoleon. Firstly, the Rev. James Row, Rector of Morchard Bishop from 1866 to 1884, had previously been a member of the 45th Foot and had fought Napoleon at the battles of the Pyrenees and Nivelle. The second link is the vine at Barton House. Tradition has it that one of the Churchills visited Napoleon while in exile. Napoleon was so grateful for the visit that he wanted to say 'thank you' with a gift, but having nothing of wealth with him, he went to the garden and gave his guest a young vine. This was brought home and planted in the new glasshouse at Barton House.

The Turnpike Trusts in the 18th and 19th centuries were a mixed blessing to Morchard Bishop. In 1753 the road from Crediton to New Buildings, Morchard Bishop, Chawleigh and Chulmleigh was made into a trust. All turnpike roads had to be at least 8 feet wide – wide enough for a cart – but, to start with, improvements were poor and it wasn't until after 1815 and the re-surfacing of the roads the McAdam way that things really did improve.

The root of the problem lay in the fact that the Crediton to Barnstaple road followed the Celtic route from hilltop to hilltop. This meant steep gradients and long travelling times (horses were changed at the London Inn). So in 1830 a new turnpike road without hills was built (the Taw Valley Road). Unfortunately it by-passed Morchard Bishop, leaving it less prosperous. The Turnpike Trusts continued to operate, gaining regular income from the stagecoaches until the coming of the railways.

The Exeter-Crediton Railway Act of 1845 formed the North Devon Railway Company in which both the Bristol and Exeter (later GWR) and the London and South Western Railway had shares. The Act stated that the railway was to be built at standard gauge 4 foot 8 inches. The Great Western Railway shareholders were in the majority and ignored the gauge ruling, building it broad gauge ($7^{1}/_{4}$ feet) instead, to link with the main GWR line at Exeter which was ready for opening by 1847. But then the LSWR gained control of the company and standardised the track again with a station at Cowley Bridge. The debate continued until the Board of Trade objected that it did not link with Exeter, so it finally reverted to the original broad gauge

The Exeter to Crediton section was eventually opened on 12 May 1851 and the Crediton to Barnstaple section was completed within three years. However, in 1860 the LSWR reached Exeter, taking control of the North Devon Railway two years later. The following year they laid a third rail so that standard gauge could run up to Barnstaple. All British tracks became standard gauge once and for all in 1892.

Morchard Bishop from the air, 1963.

Chapter 2: The Parish Council

EXTRACTS FROM THE PARISH COUNCIL MINUTE BOOKS 1896-1992

The first meeting of the Morchard Parish Council was held in the Schoolroom on Tuesday December 4th 1894 when 18 nomination papers were handed in and 11 Councillors were elected by a show of hands. Charles Mortimer of Broadgate Farm was elected Chairman.

Saturday 5th September 1896

Proposed by Mr C. Kingdon, Seconded by Mr O. Norris: That this Council is of opinion that the proceeds of this Charity is not being properly distributed, and that the Rector having charged against the account for Brandy and Wine which he has given to sick people, and declined to show particulars of his expenditure of the money of this Charity in Brandy and Wine is satisfactory. Also that the Clerk write to the Charity Commissioners explaining the circumstances of the distribution of the proceeds of this Charity, and asking them to allow this Council to appoint two additional Trustees. Carried Unanimously

May 4th 1897

Tuckfield Charity. The Chairman read a letter received from the Rev. J.C. Blackmore giving the names of the recipients of the portion of the Tuckfield Charity proceeds, which the Rector had distributed himself Proposed by Mr C. Mortimer, Seconded by Mr T. Tucker: That Mr Leach be requested as a Trustee, write to the Charity Commissioner asking them for advice regarding the irregular actions of the other Trustees, in over-riding him in the distribution of the proceeds of this charity.

November 13th 1897 at 7pm

Mr Mortimer explained that the Overseers had wanted to view the Tithe Apportionment Map and Schedule for the purpose Assessing some of the Glebe Land, and had instructed the Assistant Overseer to apply to the Rector for the loan of the Map & Schedule to be brought to the Parish Council Room to the Overseers Meeting. The Assistant Overseer had applied for the Map and Schedule, but the Rector had refused to allow it to go out of his possession, and also refused the Overseers permission to view, except during certain hours. Mr Mortimer said he thought the Rector had tried to hinder the Overseers in the execution of their work. Proposed by Mr Mortimer. Seconded by Mr Tucker: That the Rector be called upon to give up possession of the Tithe Apportionment Map and Schedule to the Parish Council and that the Assistant Overseer shall go to the Rector and request him to give them up.

14th January 1899

Tuckfield Charity. The Rev. J.C. Blackmore lately Rector having left the Parish, holding a balance of 3 pounds 9 shillings and six pence part of the proceeds of this Charity, which had not been distributed amongst the poor. It was proposed by Mr W. H. Kelland and seconded by Mr T. Tucker that the Clerk be instructed to write to the Rev. J.C. Blackmore, asking him to hand over the balance of the money to the Trustees. Carried

17th February 1904

Occupation Roads. A letter was read which had been written, and sent to the Local Government Board stating the unjust position of the Parishioners in that while contributing about £250 per annum, to the highway Rate of the District; the District Council only spend about £90 per annum in the parish, and that all the occupation roads were left without supervision or proper care and repair. The letter asked the Local Government Board for assistance to obtain redress. A reply to this was received from the Board stating they had no jurisdiction in the matter.

October 29th 1914

Preparation of List of names, The list of names of all persons serving in the Army, Navy were sent to the Lord Lieutenant. That Mr Cox be appointed to keep a record of names of those that join the Army, Navy since October 31st.

December 10th 1914
Gifts to Children. That a committee be appointed consisting of E.W. Cox, T. Smith, J. Conibeer, to obtain the names of children eligible for the Xmas gifts from the United States. Carried

Annual Parish Council Meeting, Thursday April 15th 1915
Closing of Post Office on Thurdays from 1 to 7.30pm. That this Parish Council agree to the proposed closing of The Post Office on Thursday afternoons and that the council would welcome the provision of a public call office of the Telephone Service to be erected at the Post Office Morchard Bishop.

October 6th 1917
Housing of Working classes. It was agreed that the Clerk should give the following information. Houses of Rateable value up to £8 - 180, over £8 - 12. Number of Houses not fit for habitation - 5. Number of Houses fit for habitation (void) - 8. The Council also considered that there was sufficient houses in the Parish if kept in repair.

April 15th 1918
District Nurse, That Morchard Bishop joins Lapford in providing a District Nurse.

September 28th 1918
Parish Pump. Proposed by Mr Harris and seconded by Mr Yendell: That Mr Ford be asked if he would keep the surface water from entering the well. Mr Ford consented, the Clerk was instructed to ask the Rev. H.S. Watkins if he would hand over the key so that he could enter the Wilderness.

January 3rd 1924
That the Clerk should write to the Secretary of the General Post Office saying that the Council would much appreciate the provision of a Public Telephone which is badly needed here.

December 8th 1925
Village Dump. It was agreed that a collection of Village Refuse should be made every three months, and that the Contractor should give seven days notice.

May 18th 1926
Telephone Call Office. That a 'Roll' of the people of the Parish who will act as guarantee in regard to the proposed Telephone Call Office at Morchard Bishop.

The Post Master General requires a Guarantee of £18 per year. It is estimated that the receipts would amount to £10.10s. per year.

June 9th 1931
Houses. Proposed by Mr Burrow and seconded by Dr Platt that the Crediton Rural District Council Housing Committee be written to, urging the necessity of the houses being built, as there are several applicants.

Electricity. To appeal to the Crediton Rural District Council to get the 'Ex Valley Electricity Company' to include Morchard Bishop in its scheme, for supplying the District with Electricity.

October 11th 1932
General. The Council suggested that the road from the schools to Beech Hill, which had been recently Tar sprayed should be rolled.

November 25th 1932
Unemployment. A letter from Crediton Rural District Council, asking for names and addresses of all persons in the parish who are habitually employed as Agricultural Labourers who, on the 18th November had been out of work for a fortnight, and who are likely to be unemployed between Xmas and the middle of March. The names of 15 men were supplied

June 7th 1934
Water Economy. That in view of the scarcity of water, the Clerk write to the Crediton Rural District Council, asking them to put Warning Notices to all public pumps, calling the attention of the public to the urgent need of economy in the use of water supplies.

August 6th 1935
Silver Jubilee Celebrations. That a minute be entered in the Minute Book of the Council placing on record the splendid manner in which the Silver Jubilee Celebrations were carried out in the Parish, the great harmony which characterised the proceedings throughout the day, and the brilliant weather which added so much to the day's enjoyment. God Save the King.

December 3rd 1935
Electricity Supply. A letter was read from the Electricity Company, stating that a supply for Morchard Bishop was being dealt with and would be laid as soon as sufficient applicants was received to cover expenses.

July 21st 1936
Fire Hose. In pursuance of the notice duly given at last meeting Mr Southern moves resolution on the Agenda, to the effect that when Water Supply is effective, an effort be made to provide a length of Fire Hose, to connect up to the Water Supply in case of fire.

November 16th 1936
Clerks Resignation. The Clerk tendered his resignation owing to bad hearing. The Chairman paid a splendid tribute to the faithful service rendered by the Clerk for 43 years and said that his resignation was received with regret by all. Mr F. W. Drew in a felicitous speech proposed that Mr Leach's resignation be received with great regret with many thanks for his splendid services. Mr Yendell endorsed these remarks and seconded.

8th February 1937
Clerk to Parish Council George Burrow appointed Parish Clerk. The new salary for the clerk will be £5 10 shillings per annum.

April 15th 1937
Air Raid Precautions. That Mr Tipper be appointed Warden for the Parish of Morchard Bishop.

June 8th 1937
That a Minute be entered in the Minute Book of the Council placing on record the splendid manner in which the Coronation Celebrations were carried out in the Parish, and the great harmony which characterised the proceedings throughout the day. GOD SAVE THE KING.

February 8th 1938
Central Schools. A Notice was read re the proposing of sending the elder scholars from Morchard Bishop Schools to the new Central School at Witheridge. It was stated that any 10 Ratepayers may appeal against this proposal. Mr Burrow undertook to get the necessary signatures.
Coronation Tree Planting. That one or two young Copper Beech trees be purchased and planted so as to cover the reservoir, opposite the school.

Water Supply. The Clerk was instructed to write to the Crediton Rural District Council saying the Parish Council felt that the Village Public Water Supply should be speeded up as it was a great inconvenience to villagers especially as the village wells had already been condemned. It was also causing a lot of inconvenience to the Schools where about £120 had been spent in connecting the lavatories etc. up to the main.

June 6th 1939
Water Supply. A complaint was made that certain people had been at the Public Wells early in the morning to get water for cattle.

It was decided that the people who made this complaint, be asked to keep observation for a few days and report to Mr Oatway, so that steps may be taken to stop this as the water in the Village was becoming very short.

LETTER FROM EARL FORTESCUE.
The Chairman read a letter from Earl Fortescue, Lord Lieut. of Devon, thanking him for his assistance in compiling a list of men from this Parish, who were between the ages of 18 and 38 and therefore eligible for the Territorial Army.

August 15th 1939
Evacuation Scheme. After correspondence from the CRDC was read, Mr Haydon of Woodgate was appointed PARISH SUPERVISING OFFICER. Billeting Officers were appointed for the 5 zones in the parish.

Allotment Scheme. A letter was read from Mr Chesterfield re the possibility of encouraging parishioners to grow more food in wartime by introducing more allotments and offering prizes.

The Chairman replied by saying that as there was plenty of allotment spaces available already, he did not think it would be so advantageous in the country as perhaps it would in towns.

August 14th 1940
Playing Field. The question of a Playing Field for the children was put before the Council and Councillors were unanimous that now, especially as in addition to our own children there were over 80 evacuated children with us, there should be some recognised place for them to play in.

March 28th 1945
Preparations for VE Day. After discussion it was decided to let the matter rest for the time being.

December 3rd 1946
Public Bier. The question of the provision of a Public Bier for the Parish was raised and discussed. It was agreed to ascertain prices for a Bier suitable for Morchard Bishop.

April 15th 1947
Bier. It was agreed that No. 1197A from Messrs Slingsley list be purchased for this parish the price being £37.3s.6d. plus 10% extra charge for ball bearings and carriage paid to nearest railway station. Public Seats. A letter from Mrs Rodwell, Sec. WVS was read saying that the 6 seats for the Parish had now been purchased from monies received from the Meat Pie Scheme. The seats had been obtained from Messrs Gamages of London and had now arrived.

May 6th 1947
Bier. A letter from the Rev. Doudrey was read giving the necessary permission to keep the Bier in the Church. The Chaplain reported that at a meeting of the Local Nursing Association the Nursing Committee passed a resolution offering to pay the whole of the cost of the Bier from their funds and present it to the Parish Council.

Seats. The Parish Council agreed the following sites for the seats. The War Memorial, Sunshine Lane, The Pound, Jane Way's Grave, Orchardy Gate, Barton House Corner, Entrance to the Church. March 22nd 1948.

Water Supply. The question of the very serious water shortage in this Parish was raised. The Chairman reported that the North Devon Water Board were doing their best to ease the situation.

It was their intention to utilise the Bugford Supply as soon as possible and had now tried unsuccessfully to obtain a tanker to get the water to Morchard Bishop.

December 7th 1948
Bier. The Bier had at last arrived but had been damaged in transit and would have to be repaired locally.

March 22nd 1949
Bier. It was reported that at a recent Funeral a tyre of one the wheels had come off. This was because the Bier did not have enough lock on the steering and also a handbrake was badly needed. The Chairman said he would get these things done.

December 6th 1949
Playing Field. A letter from the Social and Ex-Service Club asking for the co-operation of the Parish Council in the provision of a Public Playing Field for the Parish.

January 10th 1950
Playing Field. The Chairman read the lease of the proposed Public Playing Field (near the school) between the Heathcote Estate and Mr M. Yendell on the one hand and, the Morchard Bishop Parish Council on the other hand.

May 26th 1951
Water. The Chairman reported that he had met a representative of the NDWB who had assured him that there should be little or no trouble with the Water Supply in the future. A new pump had been ordered for Bugford and was expected to be fixed in the near future. It was also agreed that as soon as the Dartmoor supply had reached Winkleigh that the Parish Council should press for it to be brought to Morchard Bishop.

October 1st 1957
Playing Field. Mr Tipper gave a report from Brig. Barker-Benfield, Chairman of the Morchard Bishop Playing Field Committee on work done by the P.F. Committee re the proposed new Playing field in Wood Lane.

January 6th 1959
Bier. Mr S. Rice very kindly offered to store the Bier for one year from January 1959. This offer was accepted, and that if at the end of this period the bier was not used the Parish Council should sell it.

Special Meeting held on February 10th 1959. Development Scheme for Old Rectory. The Chairman read a letter from a firm of prospective purchasers of the Old Rectory. Their three schemes are as follows:- (1) Construct 30 new houses. (2) Construct 100 one roomed chalet bungalows and use the existing house for dining and recreational purposes. (3) Convert the existing house into a Hotel. On a show of hands the first option was carried.

October 11th 1960

Bier. Mr S. Rice reported that it was well over the stipulated 12 months that had been agreed to store the Bier and during that time it had not been used or enquired about. The Council decided it should be advertised in the Church magazine.

December 3rd 1963

Vandalism. A letter from the National Association of Parish Councils asked for details of any Vandalism in the Parish, and how much it cost the Council in 1962-3. It was agreed to answer that there had been no vandalism in Morchard Bishop.

September 1st 1964

Greenaway Housing. As there did not seem to be much progress regarding the promised new houses on the Greenaway estate, Mrs Watson was asked to make some enquiries at the CRDC meeting. Bier. Mr Rice asked to have the Bier removed. He was told that as the bier is no longer used he should knock it up for firewood.

February 14th 1967

30 MPH speed limit. A letter was read from Mr P. Mills M.P. in which it appeared that the Ministry of Transport were under the impression that a 30mph speed limit already existed in the village.

15th July 1980

Gardening Club. The local gardening club asked if they could clean up the old pound and plant flowers and shrubs etc. to improve the place.

September 12th 1983

Proposed closure of Middlecott Lane. This matter was fully discussed by the Council, and it was agreed that every effort should be made to keep open this lane which has been a public thoroughfare since well before living memory...

May 14th 1984

Retiring Gift to Mrs Wheeley. Proposed by Mr C. Hutchings and seconded by Mr R. Parkyn that a donation of £6.50 from the Parish Council be made towards the gift of a Garden Seat for Mrs Wheeley who was retiring after many years as Chairman of the Memorial Hall Committee.

March 5th 1990

Appointment of Clerk. The Chairman reported that the sub-committee formed to interview for the post had appointed Mrs Nott of Chulmleigh Road at a salary of £350 per annum to take effect as from April 1st 1990. He then thanked the retiring Clerk (George Burrow) for his work for the Parish Council over a period of 53 years.

February 4th 1991

Recycling. The Clerk read a letter from The Morchard Bishop Recycling Group inviting members of the Parish Council to the official opening of the bottle bank... Also a letter from Mid Devon District Council invited a member of the council to address the Parish Clerks... on the success of the Recycling Group. Mr K. Orchard was asked to be present.

Morchard Bishop Parish Council March 1999. (Left to right) back row: Frank Yendell, Geoff Rice, Mervin Webber, Roger Quick (District Councillor), Mary Bourne, and (Parish Clerk); front row: George Down, Gill Gunn, Roger Holloway (Chairman), Leslie Partridge, Vera Gillbard, Norman Snell. Absent: Clive Eginton

Church group. Left to right: F. Yendell, E. Yendell, Rev. Williamson, F. Milton, C. Rice, W. Rice, M. Mills, S. Stals, M. Chapple, S. Roberts.

The interior of the church, showing the Victorian, double-deck pulpit which was replaced in 1951.

Chapter 3: The Church and Chapels

St Mary the Virgin.

The site of this church has been a place of worship since Saxon times, the first rector, Nicholas, being installed in 1258 under Bishop Branscombe's Patronage.

The church stands on the highest part of the village (173 metres). The tower, being 95 feet high can be seen for miles around. There is a stair turret in the north-east corner, and six bells, cast by the Whitechapel Foundry were hung in 1724. Four others were added, the last of which was in 1876. Wear, however, has taken its toll, beams have been replaced and hung in 1998, and the tower repointed.

The body of the church was renovated in Victorian times, with the addition of wooden pews and a black, double-deck pulpit which was replaced in 1951 by the present one made by H. Read of Exeter and given in memory of Thomas and Mary Oatway in 1953 (Thomas having been a long-serving churchwarden).

The original rood screen, probably 16th century, had been removed and left to decay in the basement of Beech House. This was repaired and restored in 1951 (also by H. Read). The east window (in the style of the Jacobean Sanctuary) was repaired in 1957. A letter from the Dean of York (an authority on stained glass) confirmed that it was typical of the period and of real historic value.

The church organ was built and installed in 1910 by a Captain Lindsay Garrard who retired from the Fifth Dragoon Guards in 1905 and set up an organ-building company in Lechlade, Gloucestershire. He built quite a number of church organs to a very high standard and bought all his metal pipework from Germany. In 1914 he returned to the army for the duration of the war and, although he continued in church organ building in 1918, he did not complete any more new instruments.

In 1991 Morchard's organ had one of its first thorough overhauls when a new electro-pnuematic system was installed and several other additions made, at a cost of £8000. It was noted at the time that the console had originally been at the other end of the organ and it is thought this alteration was made in the 1930s. The rebuilding was carried out by Michael Farley of Budleigh Salterton. This instrument gave particular pleasure to our organist, Hilda Tilney, who continued playing into her 90th year and was possibly the oldest organist in the country. She also kept the adult choir going, though the younger ones dwindled as their interests moved away from the village. We are now dependent on part-time organists, rather like in the 1950s when there were five in the space of two years!

In 1949 the Rev. Rushbridger was installed. These were busy times for the church and much was done to re-start the pre-war activities; Mothers Union, Sunday School, fêtes, concerts and a junior choir were set up and a new graveyard consecrated. In 1954 the new church room provided a meeting place and this was recently upgraded.

Rev. Rushbridger was the last rector to live in the large rectory, where the present Old Rectory Gardens now stand. Since the upkeep of the house and garden was a great burden, now that families were smaller, it was decided to build a new, modern rectory in Church Street. The PCC (27

The height of the tower may account for it being struck, on the north-east corner by a meteorite on 17 January 1952, causing damage estimated at £1000.

There has always been a steady band of bellringers, the oldest was Harry Bowden, who at 72 completed 60 years in 1959, and was presented with an oak model of the tower with a silver bell.

Morchard bellringers, May 1997 (left to right): John Enderson, Mervin Webber, Arthur Fidler, Stephanie Ewings, Tom Wright, Dennis Cann, Bob Davies, Bob Robinson (Capt), Sue Cann, Dave Trist and Rev. Brian Shillingford

Above: Hilda Tilney with a statue of St Cecilia at the Morchard Flower Festival, 1997.

Right: In previous years, money left to the church by wealthier landowners to help the poor of the parish, was formed into a trust and is still distributed to elderly parishioners each November. A bequest to the church and a smallholding once belonging to Dora Tucker, was donated, the rent from which formed the foundation of the D.T. fund. It was later sold and the money now provides a useful fund towards church repairs.

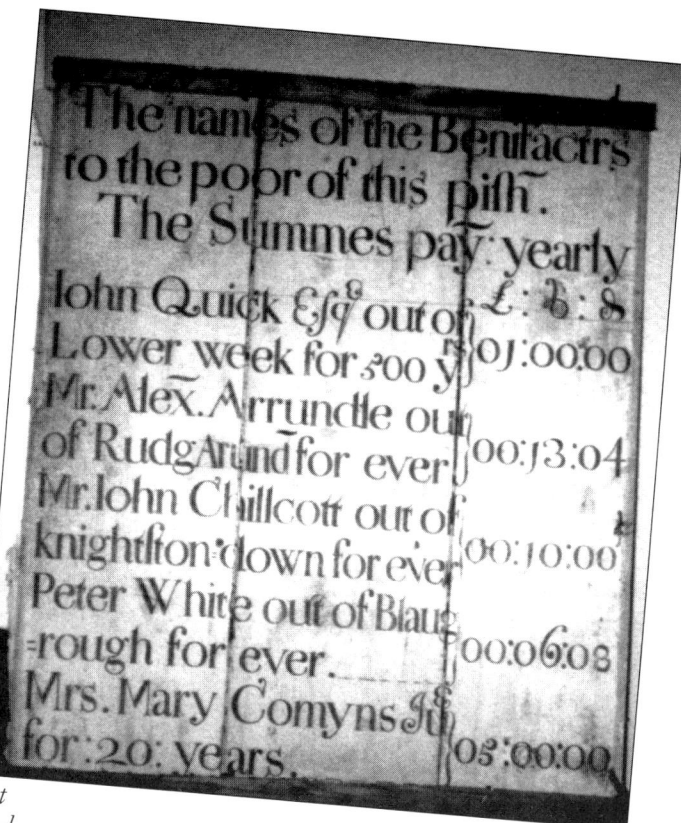

St Mary's Church Choir, 1997. Left to right: Margaret Dockings, Ida Lucas, Ruth Taylor, Jennie Holloway, Jan Pocock, Janet Symons, Hilda Tilney, Marina Down, Jean Findlay, Sonja Andrews, Pru Stopford.

The Rectory at the turn of the century.

members) agreed to contribute to start off the new Rectory fund. The remainder was raised from local events, sale of church property and grants. The blessing of this new building took place on 27 June 1954.

After Rev. Rushbridger retired in 1964 there were several rectors, but in 1975, when the Rev. Reynolds took over, Morchard was incorporated with Cheriton Fitzpaine, Down St Mary, Woolfardisworthy, Ploughill, Stockleigh English, Stockleigh Pomeroy, Kennerleigh, Puddington, Clannaborough and Washford Pyne, to form the North Creedy Group. Clergy were based at Morchard, Cheriton Fitzpaine and Down St Mary which meant a reduction in services.

Rev. Brian Shillingford came to Morchard as vicar in 1981 and when the rector at Cheriton Fitzpaine retired in 1996, took his place with responsibility of the group, which included the care of 13 parishes (now including Knowle and Sandford). Today, Rev. Shillingford has the assistance of a lay preacher, Mrs Pam Ellis.

The Chapels

In the mid 19th century, Morchard was on the edge of the Wesleyan influence from Exeter and Crediton; and the Bible Christian influence from the Taw Valley, and for a few years it had a Wesleyan Society, a Bible Christian Chapel and a Congregational Chapel. The Wesleyan Methodists appear to have had a room run by a George Northcote in Chapel lane, which still survives today and which they also used as a school. In 1907 the Bible Christian Chapel joined with the United Methodist Church.

Northcote's School had a large garden in which the Congregational Chapel was built in 1860. In 1911 this chapel was better attended and stronger than the United Methodist's but it closed in 1937, and in the 1980s Ruth and Neville Taylor had it converted into their home.

Emmanuel Chapel was licensed by James Way on 13 July 1804. He probably lived in Meadow Bank Cottage (Middle-the-Green), overlooking the village ponds. At the age of 14 he became an orphan. He was ordained in 1826 and in 1849 went to preach in South Australia, leaving his 14-year-old son Samuel to continue his education at Shebbear College. Samuel joined his father two years later and entered the legal profession there.

In 1927/8 the trustees and members of the Chapel decided to build the Sunday School Room. The existing cottage at the side, which had been occupied by the caretaker, was taken down by voluntary labour and hauled away with the help of horses and carts.

For the first time the members enjoyed conveniences, a vestry, kitchen facilities and central heating, and today the chapel is a thriving community with activities organised both in the chapel building itself and at people's homes using video and other up-to-date equipment.

The Girls' Brigade is the oldest youth club in the village having started in 1968 and other activities for young people are run, which include a 'Street Level' – a meeting place for the 14 plus.

Christian Viewpoint provides a friendly environment for up to 50 women to meet together, exchange views and consider what the Bible has to say about living today.

There are hundreds of groups all around the country, the Morchard organisation having been set up in 1992 by Liz Moles. It is now guided by a committee of Caroline Partridge, Liz Hill and Christie Bedford. Men are invited to some of the meetings!

Left: The interior of the chapel, 1999.

Below: The Methodist Chapel, 1908.

Demolishing the old cottage, 1928. Present are: Ern Edworthy, Frank Brimilcombe, Fred Yendell and Clifford Palfrey.

Re-opening the chapel on 6 May 1952, after the alterations.

The Morchard Bishop Girls' Brigade, VE Day 1995.

Sunday School outing to Northover Farm, 1943. During the war it was not possible to go to the coast.

Morchard Bishop School, 1923.
(Left to right) back row: F. Osborne, ? Greenslade, A. Tucker, D. Woodman, W. Case, O. Drew, J. Burrow, J. Chowings;
middle row: L. Rice, W. Smith, L. Woodman, A. Holland, unknown, D. Maunder, G. Chanter, M. Burrow, D. Davey, M. Yendell, E. Venner, David Tipper;
front row: ? Cann, N. Slade, N. Brailey, M. Cann, L. Partridge, K. Tipper, F. Nichols, G. Smith, A. Howard, G. Stentiford, R. Frost.

Chapter 4: School Days

The school was founded in 1733 at the behest of Mrs Thomasine Tucker. The headmaster was paid £5 per annum and the students, identified by their blue coats, were obliged to attend for two years.

At the turn of the century our church school was split into three parts; infants, boys, and girls, each group being strictly segregated and the children leaving at the age of 12 to start work. As chairman of the school, the rector was responsible for ensuring that standards were maintained and was present for the annual inspections in February. At the 1900 inspection the 21 boys and 87 girls were assessed and the school was classed as 'very good.'

School numbers fluctuated between 100 and 115 but attendance was not particularly good as children were kept home 'to nurse a baby' or 'help prepare flowers for Exeter market' and such like. But there were incentives – on 1 October 1901, for example, 19 children were presented with books as a reward for attending school every day for a month.

The school year ran from June to June but holidays were not fixed as they are today. There was usually a week for Whitsun, the harvest holiday ranged from two to four weeks, a week off for Morchard Fair week at the beginning of September, two weeks for Christmas and two at Easter. Odd days and half-day holidays were given for special events, such as the relief of Ladysmith and Mafeking in the Boer War and many of the villagers went to Crediton to celebrate the homecoming of General Redvers Buller, a hero of this conflict. Six pairs of socks were sent from the school to the Embarkation Office in Southampton, for use by 'invalided' soldiers.

Patriotism was the order of the day – a fact reflected throughout the school's curriculum, which included drill. The school was regularly closed because of snow and even rain.

Bearing in mind the poor and often cold, overcrowded housing and undernourishment, it is not surprising that illness was a regular cause for concern. Mumps, scarlet fever, measles and whooping cough were very common, as also were colds, coughs, chilblains and rashes.

The Woodwork class at Morchard School, 1927

In the spring of 1908 and January 1909 the school was closed because of epidemics of whooping cough and diphtheria. A number of cases of diphtheria, scarlet fever, whooping cough and ringworm were reported in the girls' school between 1911-13. In 1909 the head teacher was given time of because of stress.

During the 20th century the school saw many changes, but the stability of headship provided by David Tipper, followed by his son Vernon, covering a period of almost 60 years between them, was remarkable, and even for a rural area, unusual. In fact, the school was known in village talk as 'Tippers School'. David Tipper, the head from 1929, was awarded an M.B.E. in 1948 for his services to the local community and guided the school through the difficult war years.

In 1939 the school took in over 70 evacuees from Merton, near Wimbledon, who came with

33

their teachers. This made for ingenious planning: pupils did outdoor activities whenever possible and classrooms were used in rotation. During the first winter of the war, gas attacks were expected and gas masks were an essential piece of school equipment, with regular drills being held. The school still has one of the masks in its original box. That was a severe winter with much illness and when it was realised that the war would be a much longer affair than was first imagined, Merton children gradually began to return to their homes.

The pre-war period saw the school as an all-through establishment for children up to age 14, with those pupils who passed the 11-plus leaving to go to Queen Elizabeth School in Crediton. In 1945, the school became a primary school and pupils left at 11 to attend the new school at Chulmleigh.

Vernon Tipper became head in 1948, retiring in 1978. He had the first swimming pool installed across the road, as the school did not acquired its field until the 1950s. The school garden was used for gardening and hen raising. Vernon utilised his great skill as a woodwork and crafts teacher by involving the older boys in practical projects of all kinds.

In 1953, the Diocese of Exeter's Education Department arranged for extensions to be made to the school. The building acquired a hall, meals kitchen and playing field at the rear and an extra classroom at the front, making the school's facilities luxurious for the time.

The next modernisation of the building took place in 1989, by which time the number of pupils had risen to 130, necessitating provision for five classes. Since that time, numbers have fallen a little and the school currently has four classes, with the spare classroom being used by the recently-formed four-plus group, which is run by the village playgroup.

School prefects, 1930.

Above: Winners of the Chulmleigh Area Football Tournament, 1987. (Left to right) back row: Harold Harris, Michael Bourne, Philip Moore, Darren Hannant; front row: Rodney Moore, Stuart Hunt, Philip Ayre, Matthew Bailey.

Right: Tim Lyddon with children and parents in the hall in the 1970s.

In 1978 Sue Gales was appointed as Head. She writes:

I well remember the excitement I felt when I first saw our village school... its wonderful hilltop position. For a small school, it is so well endowed with its accommodation and its playing field. The 19 years in which I was headteacher – a woman head was an enormous change for a school in the first place - were years of great change

The local authority and the education departments were reorganised and various governments introduced major changes. The establishment of a National Curriculum, the devolving of financial management to schools via the governing body and the emergence of computer technology all produced a great deal of work for teachers and governors.

Somehow we managed to hang on to the vision we'd all had for a village school's pupils; to go on believing that the child is at the centre of all curriculum planning, that a diverse and stimulating variety of activities in the school produces stimulated children, and that the kind of people we need can be nurtured in a Christian-based primary school setting.

This is in accord with the foundation of the school in 1733 and the vision Thomasine Tucker had for a sound education for both boys and girls in this village.

Susan Gales, Headteacher
1978-97

The Girls' School, 1914 – Doris Yendell is in the centre of the middle row.

Infants 1933/4 (left to right) back row: Sheila Frost, Reg Land, Mabel Rice, Ronald Land, Florence Ridd. middle row: Barbara Crossman, Pearl Powesland, Hazel Howard, Mary Oatway, Betty Richards. front row: Leslie Rice, Richard Rice, Harold Stentiford, Betty Edworthy, Maurice Andrews, Frank Earle, Derek Rice.

Morchard Bishop School, 1937 (left to right) back row: Roy Rogers, Leslie Rice, Florence Ridd, Mary Oatway, Sheila Frost, Denzil Northy, Reg Lands;
3rd row: Betty Richards, Mabel Rice, Marion Greenslade, Pearl Powesland, Joan Woodley, Betty Edworthy, Joan Isaac, Phyllis Woodman, Mary Rice, Peggy Horwill, Gwen Brimilcombe;
2nd row kneeling: Cyril Cann, Henry Board, ? Lamble, Jim Greenslade, Derek Rice, Maurice Andrews, Jack Snell, Harold Stentiford;
front row sitting: Walter Ridd, O. Northy, Ronald Land, John Howard, Richard Rice.

The school in 1948.

The school, 1953: class teacher – Gwen Tipper.
(From left to right and back to front) left-hand column: David Gowen, John Crang, Derek Edwards, Betty Rice, Gillian Rice, Sandra Taylor, unknown, unknown, Stella Hunt, Timmy Hammond, Peter Moore, Bobby Brooks, Barry Leat, Hazel Brewer, Muriel Watts;
right-hand column: Fred Yendell, unknown, Graham Howard, Susan Parish, Jean Herman, Priscilla Leach, unknown, David Stone, Mary Street, unknown, Winnie Yendell, Roy Webber, Michael Hilliard, Mary Hitchcock.

Sketch by Julie Page: Morchard School at the end of the twentieth century.

1990 (left to right) back row: Michael Graves, Joanne Eastman, Adam Hooper, Helen Kaye, Emma Denford, Joanna Orchard, Bo Vanrijbroek, Sophie Howard;
third row: James Becker, Stacey Hunt, Andrea Sheen, Anne-Marie Bourne, Tonie Sandford, David Haynes, Zora Stainton, Charlotte Beddoes, Jamie Reddaway;
second row: Mrs Gales, Carl Jacobson, Claire Richards, Rebecca Sandland, Katherine Hill, Katie Elsworthy, Rachel Chappell, Tom Oxley;
front row: Jeffrey Critchley, Julian Robinson, Dominic Le Bredonchel, David Howard, James Diamond.

The teaching staff, 1999.
(left to right): A. Palmer (headteacher), S. Martin (teacher), S. Stockley (teacher), S. Thresher (teacher), S.K. Burton (deputy headteacher), J. Amor (classroom assistant), J. Howard (classroom assistant), E. Hill (classroom assistant), J. Rowcliffe (school administrator).

School days, 1997

1997 (left to right) back row: Mrs J. Howard, Matthew Curtis, Robbie Yendell, Lorraine Cleverdon, Gavin Lomas, Jamie Thoms, Christopher Turner, Ella Flight, student teacher;
middle row: Rachel Pettyfer, James Bruce, Simon Adams, Stephanie Roberts, Mrs S. Thresher, Richard Berwick, Jack Smart, Stephanie Sibthorpe, Lydia Roberts;
front row: Tomas Firby, Jack Lee, Alex Shapland, Francesca Venner, unknown, Rachelle Burton, Martyn Knight, Berti Tweedie, Nigel Reed.

The bellringers, 1997 (left to right) back row: Maria Beddoes, Daniel Curtis, Jonathan Bradford, Rebecca Partridge, Marguerite Harford, Kylie Hooper, Kirstie Smart, Ben Sands, Mrs Gales; (front row): Hannah Grant, Sophie Eames, Craig Padley, Paul McArdle, Jessie Beddoes, Wayne Cleverdon, Matthew Page, Lewis Oxley, Laura Heath.

THE BOOK OF MORCHARD BISHOP

School days, 1998

*1998 (left to right) back row: Mrs S. Martin, Sean Alderwick, Loren Eginton, Gavin Down, Rose Gaskell, Jamie Bradford, Mrs V. Hughes;
middle row: Anna Balsdon, Samuel Dyne, Jessica Powell, Liam Hole, Elias Crang, Harriet Logsdon, Joshua Coles, Robert Gooding, Tom Lee;
front row: Katie Leat, Amy Hole, Samantha Pollard, Samantha Brock, Anna Hughes, Alys Furby, Meghan Le Carpentier.*

*School Band, 1998
(left to right) back row: Joel Pettyfer, Rachel Partridge, Megan Tweedie, Sarah Dart, Hester Ellis and Arthur Rowley;
front row: Jodie Sanwell and Amy Jeffrey*

41

Harvest Supper in the 1950s.

Chapter 5: Entertainment and Leisure

The Memorial Hall

On 26 September 1930 a meeting was held at Barton House at which Lord Portsmouth, Dr Pratt, David Tipper and 17 others were present. Here it was announced that the plans for the hall had been approved and that a grant from the Carnegie Trust had also been approved together with a loan of £500.

In February 1931 the committee approved the lowest tender for the building of the hall, which was £2240.11s.10d., made by Mr White of 51 Crediton High Street. The foundation stone was laid on 6 May 1931 with much ceremony and the hall was opened the following November.

Since the end of the First World War the ex-servicemen had been trying to raise funds to build their own premises (with help from the central government), and it was agreed that they should have the hall's first-floor room. In the late 1970s as the number of ex-servicemen declined, this room was handed over to the hall committee.

Despite the generosity of Mrs Wheeley in the 1970s and '80s, the hall was in need of urgent refurbishment and modernisation by 1990. Led by the Hall Committee, a concerted effort by parishioners raised £8500 and although professional builders completed the majority of the work on a contract basis, quite an amount was achieved by way of the voluntary labour of builders and laymen. The sum required to complete the project was £64,000, and additional funds came from the Community Council for Devon and the Mid Devon District Council, who also made an interest-free loan.

Extensive work was undertaken, quite a lot of which was voluntary. The building was made wind and weather tight once again, all the windows were replaced, a new kitchen and toilet block were built, a play yard at the rear constructed, central heating was installed and the building was redecorated throughout. Once again the parish had a hall it could be proud of. I wonder what Doctor Pratt would have thought of all the alterations?

Following a week in which all organisations played an active part in organising a function, the building was re-opened on its Diamond Jubilee on 6 May 1991.

Above: Prior to the opening of the Memorial Hall in 1931, most of the village functions took place in the Reading Room in Fore Street. The entrance was through the archway and a door on the right, which is now blocked up.

The Memorial Hall

Morchard Bishop Remembered

The scene at the Memorial Hall after the opening of a two-day exhibition entitled: 'Morchard Memories' staged by the village Women's Institute to commemorate the 50th anniversary of the hall. On show were tools, pottery, documents, clothes and photographs of years ago loaned by villagers. Pictured here are W.I. members who helped with the exhibition. From the left: Kathleen Highland, Joan Edmonds, Marion Mills and Shirley Brewer

(Courtesy of the Express and Echo *14.11.81)*

Group taken in the grounds of Ridge House, on the day the Foundation Stones were laid for the Memorial Hall, 6 May 1931.
(Left to right) seated front row: Mrs Otton, Lady Portsmouth, Mr J. Warren, Mrs Doudney, Miss M. Comyns Tucker, Miss A. Comyns Tucker, Mrs B.E. Oatway, Mrs Mallett, Mr T. Oatway Senr, Mary Oatway;
standing: Mrs Southcott, Viscount Lymington, Mr Sid Rice, Lord Portsmouth, Rev. E. Doudney, Mrs Rice (Crookstock), Dr Pratt, Mr Buckingham, Mrs M. Edwards, Mrs T. Bennett, Mr E. Mallett, Mrs T. Oatway Senr, Mrs F. Yendell; seated on grass: Mr D. Tipper.

Lord Portsmouth laying the foundation stone.

Above: Church Street in the early 1930s before the demolition of the old cottages.

Right: David Tipper switching on the new electric heating system in the Memorial Hall in 1937, watched by SWEB rep., Col. Hammond and T. Oatway. The heating must have been a godsend for those who took advantage of the mobile cinema which visited the hall regularly the following year.

Below: 1929/30 site plan of the proposed hall.

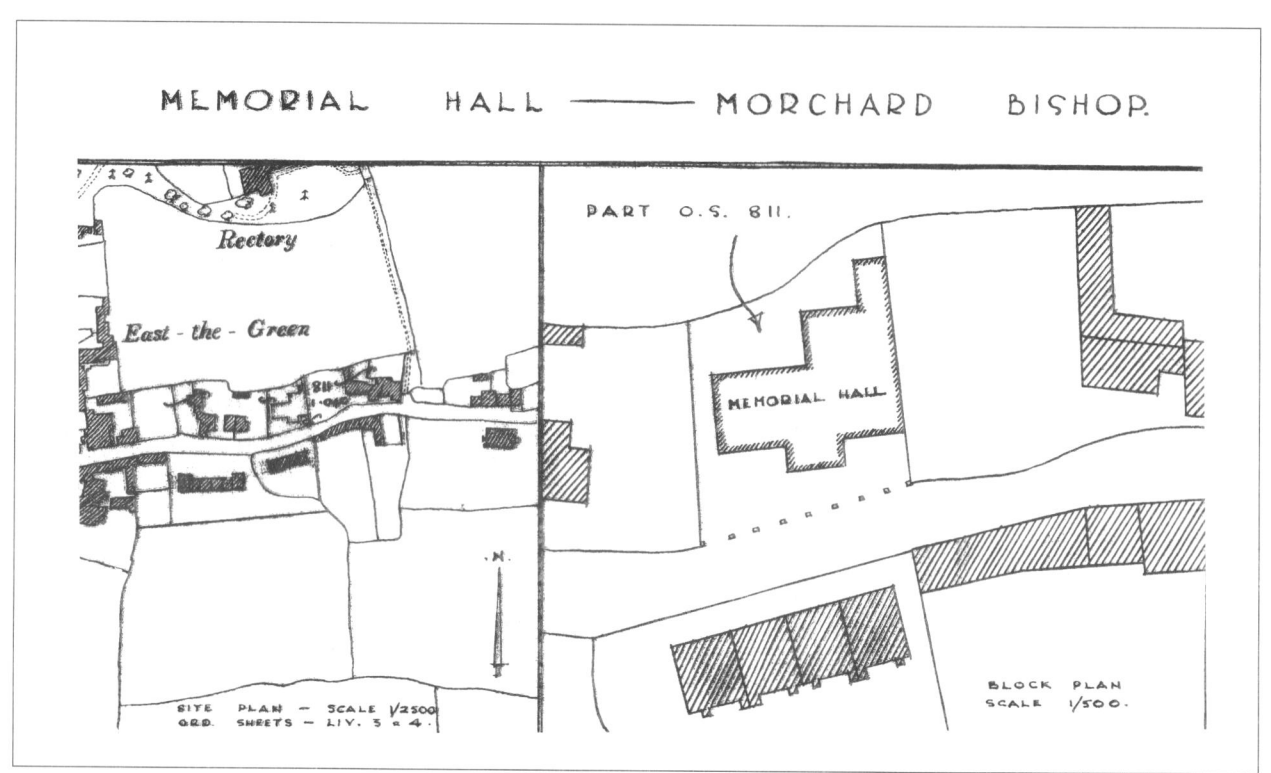

THE BOOK OF MORCHARD BISHOP

🍀 Rural Events 🍀

Dancing around the maypole at Beech Hill in the sixties.

The Carnival, October 1956.

47

Comedy and Carnival

Above: 'Allo Allo' Morchard Twinning Association float, 1989. Morchard Carnival was a regular event until the early sixties and Janice Butler and her helpers revived it in September 1989. The proceeds went to the refurbishment of the hall.

Right and bottom: fancy dress and the dancing bear at Morchard Carnival, 1909.

Below: Comic card sent from Morchard Bishop to Sussex in 1908.

THE BOOK OF MORCHARD BISHOP

Morchard On Stage

Christmas 1953
(Left to right) back row: Jack Sturgess, Harold Stentiford, unknown, Joy Mitchell, Miss Giles, Cyril Shapland, Rev. Rushbridger, G. Dockings, Ned Hooper, P. Cotton;
front row: Freda Sowden, Mary Oatway, Frank Shapland, Mrs Oliver, Miss Davie, (Joseph unknown), June Bennett, Jean Reed, Miss Hooper.

(left to right): Charlie Isles, June Bennett, Mr Giles, Mrs Mitchell, Fred Sowden, Gordon Dockings, Mrs French, Mrs North.

Village Shows

Above: Morchard Bishop 'Corps de ballet': 'The Honey Suckle and the Bees'. Left to right: Derek Hayden, David Gunn, Mike Lovell, Roger Holloway, Phil Cole, Derek Savage.

Right: Roger Holloway and Geoff Rice.

Above: Ida Lucas, who not only sang, but also produced many village shows.

Right: 'My Old Man said Follow the Van'.

Left: Humpty Dumpty, 1982.

'Snow White', December 1987.

Above: Shirley Coles as Mitzi and Jo savage as Carl; above right: Roger Holloway as Dame Natterwick.

Right: Mike Canning, Ray White and Brian Shillingford.

'Pied Piper', December 1985.
Kate Shillingford as Johnny the cripple lad, with the dancers, including: Rebecca Tapp, Samatha Kaye, Dawn Latham, Michelle Brimilcombe, Amanda Buckingham, Richard Gunn, Sarah Cook, Alison Haynes, Sheila Bailey, Jane Tucker, Andrew Holloway.

The village pram race in aid of hall restoration funds.

Parish Clubs and Organisations

The winners – Morchard Show, 1996 (by courtesy of the Crediton Courier*). Left to right: Maggie Down, Ida Lucas, Harold Webber, Matthew Page, Sid Roberts, Louisa Page, Carol Cannington-Smith, Sheila Gurl.*

Gardening Club

The Gardening Club was started in 1980 when parishioners were invited to attend the first meeting in the hall – 42 new members came to listen to John Pike of Bicton College giving advice on how to set up such a club and since then the numbers have risen to between 60 and 70 members. As well as monthly meeting, often attended by guest speakers, the club also visits various gardens and places of interest throughout the year. Its village flower and produce show has been an enduring success and is always held during the first fortnight of September, the traditional 'Morchard Fair Week'.

Bottom: The winners 1997, from left to right: Sheila Gurl, Clive Egington, Ida Lucas, Frances Preece, Gill Gunn, Ashley Baker, Harold Webber, Sid Roberts.

Below: Harold Webber with his prize-winning leeks, 1996.

The Playgroup

The playgroup was started in 1968 by Isolde Summers and Marina Down with a handful of other mothers (Pat Sandercock, Ruth Taylor and Karen Moffat). For several years all helpers were volunteers who worked for the group on a rota basis, while fundraising and handmade contributions provided much-needed equipment (which was stored in a shed at the rear of the Memorial Hall, built to house the wartime ARP fire handcart). As this was one of the first playgroups in the area, a film was made of the group to help other villages who were thinking of setting up such a scheme.

Above: Summer 1997 (Courtesy of the Crediton Courier*), clockwise: Chelsey Taylor-Haydon, Benjamin Vere, Natasha Magor, Amy Hole, Sammy Brock.*

Right: (left to right) from the top: Robert Gooding, Hattie Logsdon, Amy Hole, Chelsey Taylor-Haydon, Natasha Magor, Benjamin Vere, Anna Balsdon, Anna Hughes, Sammy Brock, Alec Gillbard, Joshua Baylis, Eloise Keatley, Luke Bradford, David Leat.

Below: 1975 (left to right) back row: David White, Tracey Hutchings, Sarah Kentish-Barnes, Duncan Scott, the Donovan twins Andrew and Philip. Seated: Nichola Down, Jason Collins, Michelle Haydon, Christine Foale, Martin Edworthy, Jessica Cotter, Carole Keeble, the Keeble twins Helen and Janet.

THE RUNNING OF THE BLACK DOG

On the evening of the first full moon each October, the following proclamation is read in the bar of the London Inn:

My Lords, Ladies and Gentlemen, since time immemorial, gentlefolk from all parts of The County of Devon, have reported their encounters with the Great Black Dog of myth, song and legend. But never more so than on the road that runs between Morchard Bishop and Black Dog.

In these parts, the sighting of the Black Dog has always been taken as an omen of good fortune, for it is believed that the Dog is the guardian of great treasure.

Tonight, as at every year at this time, we invite you to join us as we dance our own great Dog on the road to the Black Dog Inn, and join in with the music and dance that heralds the Dog's progress through the lanes.

Shortly afterwards the Black Dog will appear from the back gate of the public house where it will be pursued around the village to the accompaniment of the folk group, 'Pennymoor Singaround and Live Rehearsal'.

According to academic articles written by Theo Brown and others, the Black Dog of Devon has been sighted most commonly running along the road from Morchard Bishop to the village of Black Dog. Now it just happens that Black Dog lies alongside the Two Moors Way and close to the Mariners' Way, two footpaths that link north and south Devon. It is not beyond belief that, in days gone by, seaman from Padstow and Minehead (both famous for their 'Hobby Horses') could have called at the Black Dog for shelter and refreshment. Hence perhaps the legend was born.

Chess Club

The club which was started in 1980, meets weekly in members' houses. While most of the competition is internal, the club has played Exeter University and other local clubs.

(Left to right) standing: Howard Jones, Stephen Hargreaves; seated: Leslie Martin, Arthur Jerry, Jeff Kingaby, Withold Kawalec.

Badminton & Social Club

This club, formed in 1970/71 by a group of parents who met at the newly-formed Playgroup, proved an immediate success with about 30 people meeting on Friday evenings, to play badminton, table tennis and to socialise. The club joined the North Devon and Crediton leagues, even winning the Exeter League on one occasion.

The ceiling in the Memorial Hall was rather low and many league matches were played at Chulmleigh. The club arranged carol singing around the village and its annual fancy dress dance was very well attended by parishioners. As other organisations were formed in the village, support for the badminton club dwindled and it was reluctantly decided to wind it up in 1993.

(Left to right) top: Peter Roe, Bob Scott, Neville Taylor; bottom: Sally Slade, Annie Robinson, Ruth Taylor.

Scouts

The 1st Morchard Bishop Scout Group was formed in 1982. The first scout Section Leader was David Pocock from Lapford and a little later a Cub Pack was formed with Jennie Fawcett as its Akela. The Rector has been Chairman of the Executive Committee from the outset and Ian Penny joined the group as Group Scout Leader. Members from neighbouring parishes also join the group, which meets in the church room. At present the scout section is led by Tom Smith.

The Welcome Club

In 1989 the Welcome Club was started by Hilda Partridge and Helen Snell when 30 new members were invited to a Christmas party (above) – today it has grown to 60. During the winter months members enjoy lunches in the Memorial Hall which are cooked by members, but in better weather they organise coffee mornings at the London Inn, cream teas at various locations, and a number of outings.

The Twinning Association

St Gatien Des Bois is a lovely village in the Calvados Region of Normandy. The two villages have enjoyed exchange visits each year and many friendships have been formed, with the two villages competing in a sport (nominated by the home side) during each trip, for the Gerald Heath Memorial Cup. Gerald Heath was the first Chairman of our association and he died suddenly just before the charter was signed.

In 1999 came the 20th Anniversary of the link and a party of 50 from Morchard joined in the celebrations in St Gatien at the end of May, when a commemorative tree was planted, and a road and a square in the village were named 'Rue Morchard Bishop' and 'Square Morchard Bishop' respectively! Our French friends will join us next year to celebrate our 21st anniversary, when a tree will be planted in our village

Above: Claude Campion (St Gatien's ex-Mayor) plants a tree to commemorate the 20th anniversary of the twinning.

Left: Signing of the Twinning Charter with St Gatien Des Bois in August 1979. Left to right: Jack Wickens (President Twinning Assoc.), Geoff Rice (Parish Council), John Lucas (Chairman), Claude Champion (Mayor of St Gatien).

Below (left to right): David and Gill Gunn, John Lucas, Claude Campion, Sonia Heath and, in front, Julie Rudge and Ida Lucas in Morchard Square, St Gatien.

Young Farmers

Our Young Farmers were formed in 1945 and became a substantial organisation; paying £5 per annum membership and £1.50 for a dance or a lesson. Two of the main organisers for a while were Henry Dockings, who was Chairman, and Mary Oatway, who was the Secretary. The association closed down in 1957.

Left: (left to right): H. Shapland, F. Shapland, H. Dockings, W. Rice.

Below: Young Farmers Sheep Shearing Competition, 1950s.

THE W.I.

Our W.I. was founded in 1927 by Lady Portsmouth, who then lived at Barton House and was a personal friend of both Lady Poltimore and Lady Clinton (leading members of the county W.I). To enrol new members, Lady Portsmouth would tour the area in her chauffeur-driven car, bidding tenants to attend the first meeting in the Reading Room, which is now 'Beggar's Roost'. The annual subscription was 2s. (10 new pence) and today it is £14.50. During the 1930s, whilst it was part of the Taw Valley Group, the Morchard W.I. won the Craft and Produce Shield outright and, on returning triumphantly home, were greeted by the village brass band. Outings, often by train, to such places as Fry's chocolate factory in Bristol and the Wilton carpet factory, were the highlight of the year.

The original concept of the W.I. has, despite a rapidly-changing world, remained unaltered. From its early beginnings it was chiefly concerned with rural and domestic interests and this still continues, although it has a strong voice concerning social, economic and environmental issues of the day.

Above: Planting the flowering cherry tree to commemorate the Coronation of Queen Elizabeth II, 1953.
Top: Mrs M. Partidge (Morchard Bishop's longest-serving member) cutting the 70th birthday cake with M. Tarrant (President), J. Symonds (Secretary) and J. Knight (Treasurer) on the left, 1996.

From 1939-45, they were actively involved in the war effort and sent gifts to servicemen and women from the parish. After the war they organised craft classes, teaching such skills as glove making and smocking.

Today the monthly meetings remain a social occasion, and traditional competitions like 'flower of the month' are held with invited speakers who cover such subjects as aids, genetic engineering and wildlife conservation. In the autumn of 1999 the Creedy group's bi-annual meeting was hosted in Morchard.

A wide range of activities are organised by the county, including trips to places of interest in England as well as some foreign travel. Members have an opportunity to attend residential courses at W.I. Denman College.

To commemorate the millennium, members are planting 2000 daffodil bulbs in the lanes leading to the village and it is hoped that they and the W.I. will continue to flourish in the 21st century. We remain 'Todays women working for tomorrow's world'.

Above: The Morchard W.I., 1999.
(Left to right) back row: Shirley Pope, Janet Knight, Ruth Taylor, Maureen Carr, Jean Moore; middle row: Marion Mills, Margaret Chapple, Eira Jackson, Barbara Elliott, Mary Tyler, Jean Findlay, Maureen Davies;
seated: Felicity Hutchings, Janet Symons, Audrey Frampton, Marina Down (President), Maddy Tarrant, Sheila Nadim, Muriel Hockeridge.
Absent: M. Partridge, P. Macey, L. Lamb, R. Taylor, S. Gurl, R. Hepworth and M. Shobrook.

Above: Morchard Bishop – Bishops; North Tawton Witches changing the county banner to celebrate 75 years of the W.I. Movement, 1995.

Parish map, made by W.I. members in 1995. This now hangs in the Memorial Hall.

Chapter 6: Transport and Communications

At the turn of the century the 'iron horse' was king. The London and South Western Railway line brought passengers and goods for the parish to Morchard Road, competing with horse-drawn vans, while the wealthy still enjoyed their ponies and traps. *Kelly's Directory* of 1902 *(page 12)* on Morchard Bishop shows carriers to Exeter: 'Jn Conneybeer & Matthew Wreford, on Fridays, returning same day. Carrier to Morchard Road, Frederick Howe.'

The vans were covered, with a wooden bench down each side, a straw-covered floor and a small oil lamp hanging in the corner. Produce for the market – rabbits, poultry, eggs, butter and cream would be packed in alongside the passengers, who on busy days would be squashed together so that they could hardly move. The horse, or pair, struggling up the hills, averaging little more than five miles per hour, sometimes required assistance from neighbouring farmers' horses, and blocks often had to be placed behind carts to stop them running backwards. One of the last horse-drawn carriers from Morchard was Henry Heard, a man easily recognised by his very long beard!

The Thomas family ran a service from Witheridge to Exeter, via Black Dog, Morchard and Crediton and village carriers competed for the trade. The Leach family from Morchard were well known locally as farmers, and also as carriers to and from Exeter in the late 1800s. In the 1920s Fred Leach, who was also a nurseryman at Frost, bought a second-hand Ford 14-seater bus, and started a village service to Exeter. He kept the bus at Frost on the corner of Watery Lane and in 1923 added to his service a Chevrolet touring car/taxi. He replaced the Ford the following year with a seven-year-old, ex-military 20-seater GMC. On Tuesdays the route took in New Buildings, West Sandford and Sandford, and on Fridays travelled via Morchard Road and Copplestone competing directly with Thomas Brothers, the journey taking nearly one-and-a-half hours.

The buses carried a large number of parcels including medicines from the wholesale chemist in Exeter, and such items as china and glass. Timber was carried on the roof of the bus for the village blacksmiths, carpenter and undertakers. Roger Grimley in his book *Wheels around Witheridge*, pictures a dark, wet winter's night:

An unknown lady outside the post office (now 'Woodstock'), at the turn of the century.

By the dim light of an acetylene cycle lamp, the slippery rungs of the ladder at the back of the bus would be climbed and the tarpaulin pulled back. All the time, as Charlie Bryant remembered, "the wind would be blowing hard enough to darn near cut your head off", tugging at the ropes and blowing the cover off while the driver or parcel boy groped about trying to find the correct bit of wood for the customer.

There were still local horse-drawn carriers taking produce to market in Exeter each week (including both Mr Edworthy of New House, and Fred Rice, Norman Rice's grandfather). Mr Yendell senior remembers one such owned by Mr Connibeer who lived near Smiths the blacksmith:

One carrier would get so drunk that the pony would make his own way home, arriving about three or four in the morning. One night on his way home the carrier was stopped by a policeman in Crediton, who insisted on driving home with him, as he was very drunk. The policeman jumped up on the front of the cart, and at Dockings, just outside the village, the cart came to a halt. The carrier could not have been too drunk that night to know they were by a big pond.

"We're home now – off you jump," he told the policemen who jumped straight off into the middle of the pond as the cart drove off without him.

Fred Leach was another local carrier and his business was passed to his daughter, Alice Maud Blanche Leach, shortly before the 1930s. Alice married Mark Roberts of Farthing Park in 1931 and they continued the bus service until the following year when it was taken over by Witheridge Transport, and in turn Greenslades. In 1947 it was bought by Devon General who introduced double-decker buses but this service declined as more and more of the population bought cars.

Doctor Pratt was one of the first in the parish to own a car – the famous Model 'T' Ford, which was driven by a chauffeur. In the early 1920s, George and Joe Burrow owned a 1925 Singer two-seater with a 'Dickie' seat at the back. They sold that and bought a 350cc Triumph motor cycle combination and then a famous 'Bull Nosed Morris'.

The first petrol pump was installed at Drew Brothers on Polson Hill but the Burrow Brothers stored petrol in two-gallon cans in the old skittle alley behind their shop, and probably had as much as 70 gallons stored there at a time (the Petroleum Regulations did not come into force till later). They bought it at 7d. per gallon but Shell produced a better quality brand that cost 10d. It was not until the mid 1930s that Aubrey Snell started the first garage in what is now the London Inn skittle alley.

Morchard Bishop Bus Garage.

Above: Bill Thomas of Witheridge with one of his buses.

The fate of an out-of-control tractor on Spire Lake Hill.

Left: A Devon 'ship' waggon, characterised by the spindles on the sides, and the high back which gave it its name. Built by John Reed of Morchard Bishop c.1870 for Mr George Way of Ashley Farm, Thorverton, it was passed to his brother-in-law, Mr Charles Hawkins, who preserved it until his death in 1968 when it was aquired by Tiverton Museum. The waggon would have been used for carrying sacks of corn to the local mill and for work in the harvest field. For hauling particularly heavy loads, the driver would have used an extra horse, or 'fore' horse, at the front.

(Photo by kind permission of Tiverton Museum.)

From the Partridge Collection

clockwise from top left: 1955 Ariel 650cc Hunt-master; 1958 3½-litre Mark I Jaguar; 1934 20hp Sunbeam owned by Roger Carter of the Post Office since 1934; another vintage Sunbeam visiting Morchard Bishop's twin town of St Gatien Des Bois in Calvados, Normandy.

Doctor Pratt with his chauffeur-driven Rolls Royce leaving the Lodge (now The Parks).

Telecommunications

By the early 1900s the Electric Telegraph System was well established throughout the United Kingdom and telephones were coming into general use in Plymouth and Exeter.

The telegraph system that had been introduced from 1837 enabled messages to be sent by Morse code to a network of post offices throughout the country and the world. Joe Burrow, whose father owned the tailor's shop (and Post Office after 1914) can remember them employing a live-in man to take down Morse Code and transcribe it. before giving it to the telegraph boy who would then deliver it to its recipient:

I was the Telegraph Boy for years and I used to deliver telegrams on a bicycle. We got one (old) half pence for under half a mile, three pence for over half a mile and six pence for up to half a mile and then a shilling over a mile. If it was over one-and-half mile we had to collect six pence from the recipient. Sometimes if it wasn't good news they wouldn't pay. The first time I heard the radio was in 1932 when I cycled out to West Aish with a telegram for old Mrs Mortimer. Her granddaughter answered the door and I met her for the first time. She was just 16 and I later took her to the village dance. We now have been married nearly 50 years. We had the first telephone in the post office. There was just one line and it went to Copplestone, Morchard, Lapford and other post offices. It also went to Morchard Road railway station. You had to turn the handle four times for Morchard Road and five rings for Morchard. Sometimes it got confusing as to the number of rings and people got very upset.

Parish Council minutes record requests to the Post Office for a public call office in 1915, 1924 and again in 1926. The two kiosks outside the present Post Office and at Frost were not installed until after 1936.

A Morchard Postman in the early 1900s.

The village Postmistess, then Anne Henwood, presents Freda Heggadon with a rose bowl and certificate to mark her 31 years as the village Postwoman, 1978.

Postal Service

In and after the First World War the Royal Mail horse trap used to come from Crediton to the present Post Office where all the mail for Black Dog, Kennerleigh, Washford Pyne, Worlington and lots of other villages was sorted and from where it was then delivered.

In the mid-fifties the village Post Office was taken over by Fred Sowden who transferred the business, first to a council house in Fore Street and then once again to 'Woodstock'

Prior to the present postal delivery service coming into operation in 1978, whereby vans delivered to all areas, all deliveries of post were made on foot, with deliverers walking many miles a day in all weathers. For this they were paid for three hours per day, six days a week. Freda covered the village; her father, Fred Sowden, covered Dinneridge, Redhills, Wigham and Middlecott; Tom Partridge covered Broadgate, Aish, Knightstone, Crookstock and Scotland; and Harry Bowden covered Frost, Woodgate, Southcott and Oldborough.

The Post Office was to return to its present location in the early eighties when it was taken over by Helen and Norman Snell, and in the mid nineties Steve and Roger Carter, who had once owned Polson Hill Garage, took over the service.

Chapter 7: Farming

As the twentieth century opened, farming was still suffering from the great depression which had hit the whole of Europe in the 1870s, when the great prairies of North America flooded the market with grain. This continued right through to the 1930s, although home output grew in the First and Second World Wars when U-boats sank the supply ships and everybody was encouraged to 'dig for victory'; every scrap of land was used to produce food and farmers were given incentives to increase their yields. Mary Richards recalls:

My Father, Thomas Oatway, was born at Hill Farm in 1897 and remembers the ruin of the old farmhouse that had burnt down in the early 1890s. In 1908 when my great grandfather died, they had to carry his cortège across the fields via Lane End to the church, because the lane was in such a bad state of repair after the rebuilding of the farmyard and house. My father retired in 1955 and moved into a new house in the village.

Harvesting at Brownstone.

There was some relief for local farmers in the 'hungry thirties' when the Ambrosia factory opened at Lapford which traded with the new Milk Marketing Board and bought the milk at steady prices. This was particularly appreciated by the farmer's wives who no longer had to produce butter and cheese on their farms.

By the end of this decade most of the large estates, such as Lord Portsmouth's at Barton House and Comyn Tucker's at Beech Hill, had been sold off – many to their tenants. It is interesting that while there were nearly 60 farms in the parish in 1939, today there are only two dozen. (See *Kellys Directory* for 1939, *page 13*).

Post-war government policies and membership of the ECC, which came in 1973, improved farming incomes, although the BSE crisis has been the cause of very anxious times.

Although some local families have farmed the same land for 80 or 90 years, the Tuckers of Langland Farm have been in residence since the 1600s and for all or most of this time they have been the owners. The local family tradition nearly came to an end in 1891, when Emma Maria Tucker was widowed. Later on, three of her four sons left but Hedley took over the farm and was succeeded by Henry who is now retired and lives nearby. His son Royston is preparing for his own son Andrew to take over in the next century.

George Henry Cousins moved to Oxenpark in 1878 and was succeeded on the farm by his son, Francis George Cousins (1892-1968), an early pioneer in the use of tractors for farmwork. His wife, Alice Gertrude (née Luxton), died in childbirth in 1936 and their children, Gertrude Mary and Francis George Henry Cousins, took over until 1999, when Stephen North replaced them, he being the fourth generation to farm the land.

The Elworthy family moved from near South Molton into Higher Weeke before 1915, and still farm it today. The Pugsleys were another old, locally-established farming family at Maer Farm until 1993 (the farm appears as 'Mare' in *Kelly's Directory*). In 1926 the Shaplands moved into Shobrooke farm, and are still going strong. This is our only Domesday farm in the parish.

Fred and Annie Yendell arrived at Wood Barton in 1911 from Bratton Fleming. Their son Frank took over the farm and was succeeded by his son Frank (junior). A cousin wrote the following graphic description of the move:

Morchard Bishop Dairy Class held in the Drill Hall, April 1915.

Dig for Victory; part of the school grounds was turned into an allotment (Wood Barton Farm can be seen in the background).

Plans were made to make the main move in the autumn of 1911. In late October, my father, then a boy of eight, and his uncle, Richard Chammings, set out with the flock of Closewool sheep, completing the 15 mile journey to Mr Gill's farm at Great Hele in a day. Fortunately for the family Great Hele was situated approximately halfway between Sprecott and Wood Barton, thereby making a convenient and essential breaking point in the journey.

The first day's journey with the sheep had gone well, with the flock settling to a steady pace after their initial excitement at being loose on the road... arrived at Great Hele in good time. My grandfather had ridden from Wood Barton to meet them, stay the night at Great Hele, and help them on the second day as neither my father nor Richard Chammings knew the way

The second day's travelling soon became irksome. The dogs grew tired, people grew hoarse with coaxing on the dogs and sheep, the sheep slowed their pace and developed lameness, the very lame being loaded into a cart brought along for the purpose, and all too soon the daylight began to fade. It was almost dark when the weary party arrived at the edge of Wood Barton where the flock was turned into the first available grassfield. Horses and dogs were stabled at the farm and the drovers put up at Mrs Steer's in Morchard Bishop, my grandfather doubtless turning over in his mind the not altogether flattering remarks which bemused onlookers had made about the size of his ewes as he passed by.

The following day my father saw Wood Barton for the first time in daylight and after a quick look around the place gathered up some choice apples from the orchard to take home, although I suspect that more than one was eaten on the long homeward journey.

Two weeks later on 11 November 1911, the main move was made with many neighbours volunteering to help out in the adventure with carts and wagons. A special double-shafted furniture van was hired from Barnstaple for the contents of the farmhouse. All the loading was feverishly completed so that by the evening of November 10, 31 assorted carts, wagons, ladder carts, traps etc., were let down on the long grass verge of the road opposite the now disused Stowford Chapel, ready for the horses, and an early start the next morning. The cattle were to be moved on the same day on the first half of their move, as far as Great Hele. Richard Chammings and his helpers set off very early in the morning encountering few problems, although my father who was to help them, and who had spent the night at nearby Thorne Farm because Sprecott was packed up, overslept. After eating a very hurried breakfast he ran across the fields to catch up.

The route taken by the cattle followed that taken earlier by the sheep. From Stowford Cross, south over Bratton Down, descending the Bray Valley to South Molton, and the break at Great Hele farm on the south side of the town. On the second day the drovers set off with their animals on the Witheridge road as far as Meshaw, where they turned off to follow the most direct road to Morchard Bishop through East Worlington and Three Hammers. The roads here were, in places, too steep and narrow for the convoy of horsedrawn vehicles to negotiate. The convoy therefore took the better though longer route through Meshaw to Witheridge, Thelbridge, Black Dog and finally Morchard Bishop, though this did not prevent one particularly well-laden wagon from demolishing some railings at the foot of an incline, for which my grandfather had to pay.

The market cart which my grandmother was driving was laden with food for the whole party of helpers, who stopped to eat their lunch and rest the horses for only a short break, before setting off again in the hope of reaching Wood Barton before nightfall.

Finally, in the evening, in pouring rain, tired and bedraggled they arrived in the yard at Wood Barton. It was raining too heavily to unload very much so the horses were let out and stabled and the women, by previous arrangement went over to Morchard Bishop to spend the night. The men gathered in the cold farm kitchen where they soon had a fire going in the huge hearth, brewed up some tea, and pulling their makeshift chairs as best they could to the warmth of the fire, slept in their clothes. The family cat who had come with them soon caught so many mice in the empty house, that he too curled up by the fire and fell asleep. The move was accomplished.

Fred Yendell aged 67, taken in 1932 when he was judge at the Devon Cattle Breeders' Show.

Morchard Bishop School Poultry Club, 1939.
Standing row includes: J. Howard, B. Richard, C. Burrow, J. Isaac, M. Oatway, ? Lamble, C. Lamble (two of the club members in this row are unknown);
front row (left to right): R. Rice, P. Isaacs, J. Snell, L. Rice, J. Wills, C. Burrow, H. Webber, R. Rogers, Ron Land, M. Andrew.

Above: Emma Maria Tucker

Left: Hedley Tucker and son Henry at Langland Farm with Devon herd, 1930s.

Francis George Cousins on his Case tractor in 1938.

A Tasker traction engine built in 1899.
Left to right: Ned Davey, Ern Delve, Oliver Drew and Chas. Smith. (Photo taken by Albert Pugsley.) This engine was first owned by V. J. Elson of Copplestone, who sold to Fred Cann of Morchard, after which it was bought by James Elston in 1921. It was broken up in 1928.

Long Service on the Farm

Most farmers today manage with just themselves and their children working the land, relying on contractors when necessary. In the early part of the century however, there were probably 40 or more agricultural workers in the parish. In general, they were a dedicated bunch, some of whom worked for over 40 years for a single employer. Gilbert James was a well-known local figure who worked at Brownstone Farm for Farmer Hill and later the Wedlake family for nearly 50 years, retiring at the age 70. He always ploughed with horses, never with tractors. He had five daughters, one of whom, Louie, worked at Brownstone for 32 years. What a useful person she must have been because in addition to the housework, she milked the cows, fed the calves, poultry and chickens. She is still actively employed in the parish.

Another loyal worker was Aubrey Edwards who, on leaving school at 14, worked for Thomas Oatway at Hill Barton and when the farm was sold in 1955, went on to work for Frank Gillbard. He retired in 1980 after 47 years. Likewise, Wilfred Rice, a well-known and much-loved Methodist preacher, lived and worked for no less than 40 years at Easton Barton

Above and left: Louie James with her father at Brownstone in the 1930s. One of her many jobs was to care for the chickens.

Above: William Watts receive his long-service certificate. He worked for Mr and Mrs Fred Yendell, first at Bratton Fleming and then at Wood Barton, for 63 years. His son worked at Wood Barton from the age of 14 until his retirement through ill health at the age of 63.

Left: Young Aubrey Edwards

Below and bottom left: Gilbert James and his certificate for 49 years and 3 months service at Brownstone Farm.

Above: Haymaking at Brownstone, 1930s. Louie James appears to the right of the picture. Also present: Maurice Wedlake and Gilbert James (centre).

Left: Frank Shapland, W. Watts and 'a lot of bull'.

Right: The old farmhouse at Scotland Farm, 1937.

A roundhouse mechanism, now in Tiverton Museum. Horses walked around the mechanism to provide power. (Picture courtesy of Tiverton Museum).

Mervyn Rice at Ridgeway Farm. He recalls:
'One of my earliest memories was going to visit relations at Healand Farm at weekends and helping with the thrashing which was done with a horse-drawn thrasher. My job was to keep all four horses moving in a roundhouse.

A workman's trip to Ilfracombe, July 1924. Charles (Karl) Mortimer and some of his employees setting off on their annual farm outing from West Aish Farm. His Father, Charles Mortimer, farmed Broadgate and later Aish, Watcombe, Knightstone and Venn, which he handed on to Karl. (Charles Mortimer was the first Chairman of the Morchard Parish Council.).

Harry Dockings with his binder. The Dockings Family took over Southcott Farm in 1915 and purchased it in 1950. His grandson Gordon and his two sons now farm it.

Barton House

No review of farming in Morchard would be complete without mentioning the Earls of Portsmouth and their estate. The 5th Earl lived at Eggesford House and, according to the minutes of the Morchard Bishop Church Restoration Committee, was very influential in local matters of planning and building. Barton House (pictured below in 1999) was built by the Churchill family in the 1830s, when Lady's Plain was built, although the 6th and 7th Earls preferred to live mainly at Eggesford or Hartsbourn in Hampshire. Eggesford House was not used after 1911. The 8th Earl, Oliver Henry, and Lady Portsmouth came to live in Morchard in 1926, and they soon became involved in the community. About this time the Morchard and District Nursing Association and the Women's Institute were set up and they were very much involved in the planning of the Memorial Hall which was opened in 1931. They employed a butler, a chauffeur, a lady's maid, gardeners, estate woodsmen and several extra female staff. They installed electric lighting, driven by an engine, and made numerous alterations and improvements to both the house and the farm.

The era came to an end following the death of Lady Portsmouth on 11 May 1938 and in the following year the Earl moved back to Farleigh Wallop. Both he and his wife appear to have been very well liked and respected by the community, but shortly afterwards he returned to the United States where he died. In July 1939 most of the estate was auctioned off at the Rougemount Hotel in Exeter. It comprised Barton House, Wood Barton Farm, Hill Farm, Morchard Wood (withdrawn and sold later), Broadgate Farm (149 acres), Broadridge Farm (145 acres), Healand (82 acres) and other small pieces of land. Quicks Hill Cottage was sold to a Mr Risdon for £195.

Barton House was commandeered by the army for the duration of the war and then for a short time housed several homeless families. It was unoccupied until 1953 when it was bought by Mr and Mrs Yendell (snr), who restored both the house and the surroundings to their present high standard.

BERT BRIMILCOMBE RECALLS:

We used to plough an acre a day but we walked about 8 miles doing it. Jim Ford, who used to live at Trelawney and later at Crockers was one of the village rabbit trappers and he paid various farmers so he could trap the rabbits twice a year, but not in the summer when the young rabbits were being bred. We boys used to work for him and he would pay us 6d. (old money) for each rabbit we caught. We used to set gin traps and snares and he would shoot some. Sometimes we would collect 50-60 rabbits a day. We would gut them straight away but leave the skins on and then tie them in pairs (head to foot) and they would hang on bars in a big hamper, that could carry up to 20 rabbits. Twice a week he would take these carcasses on his horse and cart to Morchard Road Station and put them on a special rabbit train, which ran from Barnstaple to Exeter, stopping at all stations. A firm from Crediton, W.Gilbert, also used to come around by road and collect these.

This trade came to an end in 1954 with the advent of myxomatosis that killed 99 per cent of the rabbit population. About the same time the gin trap became illegal. This was a cruel way of catching them but it was the way of the countryside at that time.

Left: Fred Sowden with his steam locomotive and thrashing machine. He was later appointed village Postmaster and moved the Post Office into a council house in Church Street. When he bought 'Woodstock', he moved the Post Office back to where it had been in 1914.

Below: Thresher party, 1941, thrown to celebrate Harvest Home at North Leigh. Around the table are Mr and Mrs Dymond, Mr Wood, George Greenslade, Francis Andrew, Bonjo Greenslade and, on the far right, Sid Smith.

Left: Mucking out the hard way – Maurice Wedlake and Joe Bradford, the Black Dog postman.

Below: Sheep shearing

Below left: Snowbound in 1978, Sandra Wedlake and Clare Duckworth.

(Left to right) front row: Maurice Wedlake, Bob Cann, Charlie Couch, Jack Hill;
back row: Fred Pugsley, Ern. Isle, Ken Nott, Tom Wedlake, Ken Gillbard.

Middle and West Aish

Middle Aish

Situated on a gentle southern slope in the far south-western corner of the parish, Middle Aish may have been the parent of the present hamlet. Any precise dating of the wonderful old roof of this former farmhouse is difficult, but the late Charles Hulland suspected it to be early 15th century.

In 1978 the house was in a bad state of repair and was bought and restored by Tony and Sheila Gurl. It is now owned by Tony and Alison Kilburn.

Above and right: Middle Aish, May 1979, and nine years later in 1988.

West Aish

This house was built in three stages, the first part probably in the 1500s, with a later cob extension and then an impressive Regency addition in the mid 19th century. Previously known as Hart Ash or West Ash, the name Aish seems to have been changed around the turn of the century. It is now owned by Diana and John de la Cour.

Above and left: West Aish House, 1998 and a drawing of West Aish Farm.

Stone Ash

STONE ASH

This building began life as an open hall house in about 1500 with its hearth in the middle of the hall. It had a cross passage and lower room, the roof was thatched and some of the original thatch survives over the hall, still tied with twisted willow, and smoke-stained. A parlour with solar above was added in around 1570 and 60 years later, a chimney, stairs, flooring and new windows.

In 1971, the house was bought by George and Dolly Matthews, who laboured long hours carrying out extensive alterations and refurbishment. It is now owned and occupied by Ron and Jan Pocock.

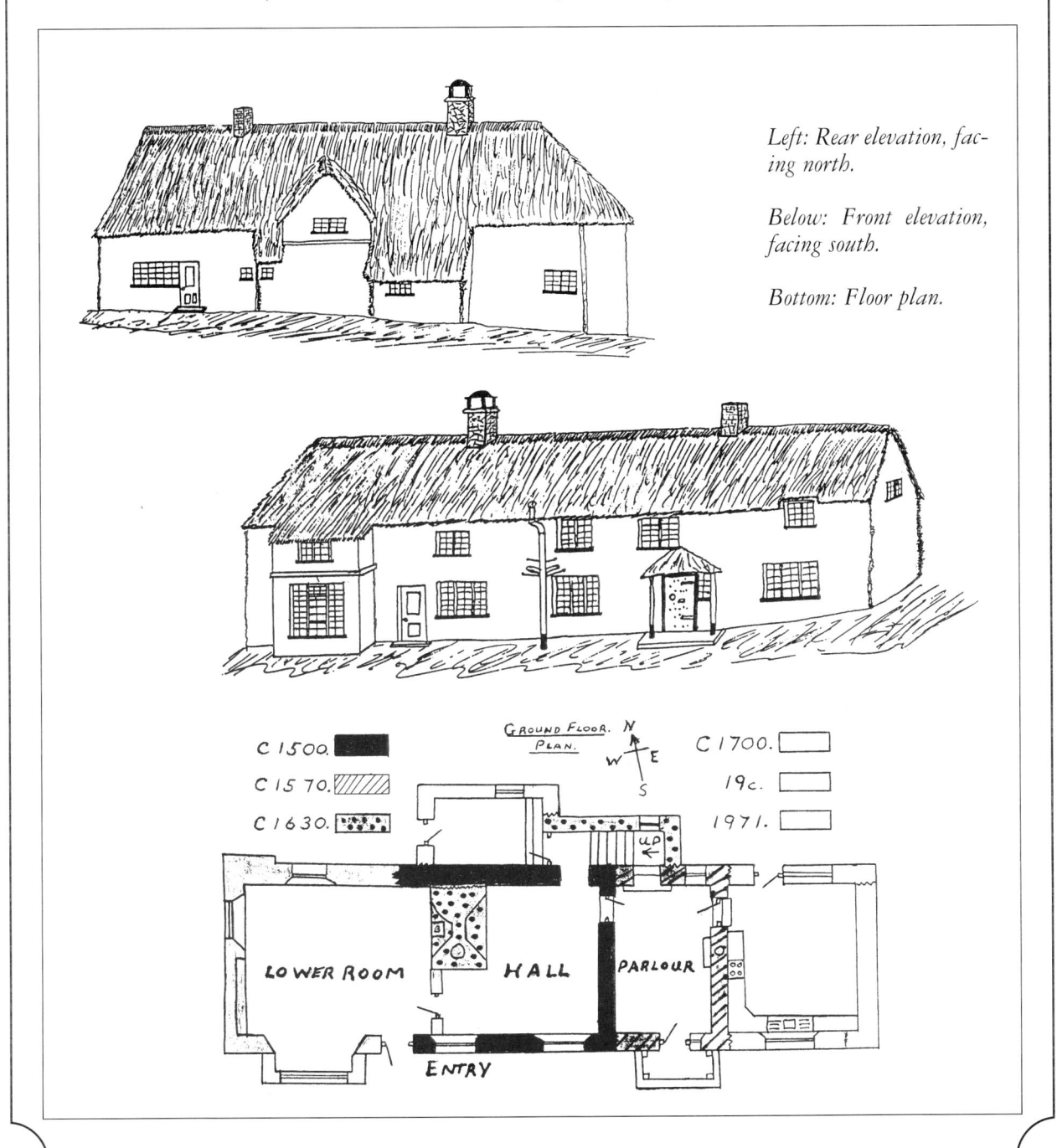

Left: Rear elevation, facing north.

Below: Front elevation, facing south.

Bottom: Floor plan.

Rudge Farm

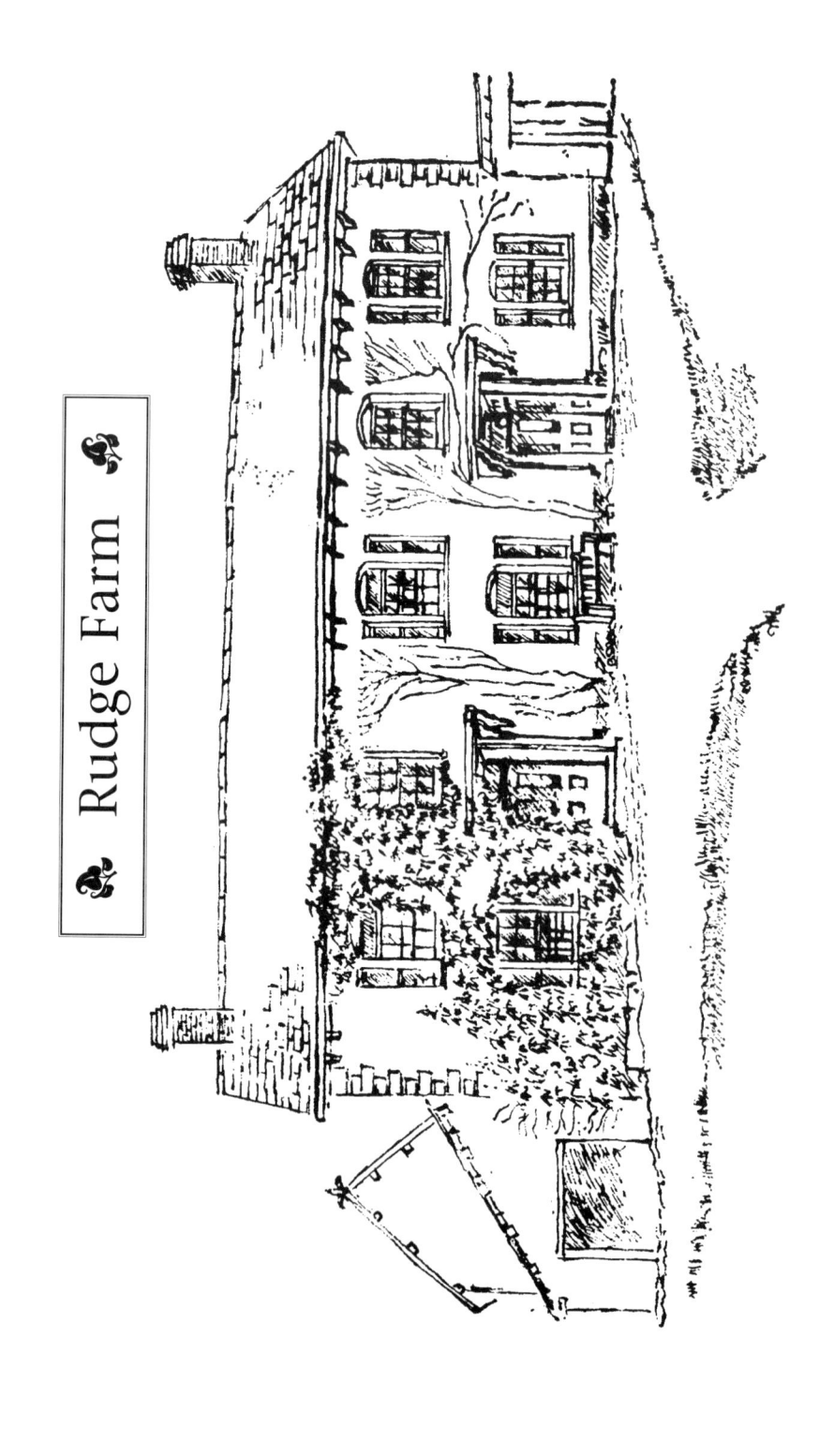

When viewed from the south, Rudge gives the impression of being a superior, mid-19th century house. This is a complete masquerade – the house is probably at least 550 years old. It occupies an isolated position in the south-west of the parish. To the south an ancient track, which has recently become known as Windmill Lane, follows the line of an east-west ridge, probably accounting for the name of the site which dates back to the 1300s. The main house is built almost entirely of stone although the tops of the walls have about a foot of cob probably dating back to the 19th-century re-roofing. The wings are of cob. The roof is described in *Buildings of England* by Bridget Cherry and Nikolaus Pevsner as 'Devon's carpentry at its best.' The house was thatched in 1852 and is owned and occupied by Marion and David Mills.

Easton Barton and Sidborough

EASTERN BARTON

This mainly stone-built house (*above*) dates from the early 16th century and was built by the Easton family who lived there until around 1630. It has an early Tudor door frame with a screen passage of the hall and a turret staircase at the west end. The family were strong supporters of the Roman Catholic Church and helped pay for the new aisle of the parish church.

When Henry VIII dissolved the monasteries, the family built a chapel in a back bedroom of the house where they worshipped and, in 1587, they were fined by the court on several occasions for failure to attend church. The house is currently owned and occupied by Marcia and John Poole.

SIDBOROUGH

Sidborough is Grade II listed, being of historical and/or achitectural interest typical of most cob and thatch houses in Devon dating back to the 17th century. Constructed c.1640, it still has the original 'A' design roof-frame, deep lap joints and shallowed, trenched purlins with the ridge spliced and ties pinned. The protruding pegs in the roof frame are the trademark of local craftsmen.

Fortunately, the main parts of the house, cob walls, internal plaster, lathe ceilings and wooden beams, have been kept intact. An interesting feature is that the thatch on the road side contains the original base laid in 1640 with the rye which was used by thatchers until the end of the 17th century. In recent years a sword was found amongst the old thatch in the roof which is thought to have been hidden during the Civil War, possibly when Fairfax's army marched past on their way to Torrington. The house is currently owned and occupied by Mary and Mark Tyler.

Beech Hill

Built in 1707 and restored in 1810, Beech Hill was extensively rebuilt in 1896. The owner, the Rev. Charles Comyns Tucker, was Lord of the Manor and Rector of Washford Pyne with the hamlets of Higher and Lower Black Dog. He sold off most of his land in the 1850s.

Since 1983 Beech Hill has been the home of a group who set up an intentional community there. The residents have changed over the years but the community is still thriving and today 23 people at the property, ranging in age between 6 months and 66 years!

The object of the community is to live in harmony, and pool energy and resources. Some of the residents work outside, others inside, some rent accommodation and others lease. Most eat together each day. The focus of Beech Hill is mainly ecological and involves many parish activities, such as the running of the highly successful Community Composting Scheme.

Above: Beech Hill residents and friends celebrate planting rare, west-country varieties of apple in the orchard.

Below: Beech Hill House, 1999.

Population and Habitat Change

As more rural dwellers emigrated or moved to the towns, rural depopulation, which started in the 1870s, became a problem. In 1851 Morchard's population was 1854 (only 41 were entitled to vote), and by 1961 this had dropped to well under half, at 780. By 1981 numbers were up again to 924 and although up-to-date figures are not available, today there are 761 people over 18 on the Electoral Roll who are eligible to vote, suggesting a slight increase in the overall population since 1981.

This has been due, in large part, to people moving away from the towns to enjoy the beautiful and peaceful countryside of the area. In many cases they occupy not only the large farmhouses, which are no longer required (the number of farms having declined), but also the derelict farm buildings which have been converted into homes. These old stone and cob barns were no longer suitable for modern farming methods and many now serve as holiday cottages to provide farmers with a very useful second income.

The hamlet of Aish is a good example. In 1953 West Aish Farm, which was described, 'As one of the best farms in the county of Devon' was sold by auction at Exeter for £14,000. This included 144 acres of land, the farmhouse with seven bedrooms, two cottages and the farmyard. By 1976 the land had been sold off to adjoining farms, the main house, because it had deteriorated, was sold off at a knock-down price, and the very derelict farmyard sold as a ruin. The lovely old 14th century house and smallholding at Middle Aish had become unoccupied and partly derelict. Today these two stunning old houses have been restored as private residences and the farm buildings are now a holiday self-catering complex, which hundreds of tourist have enjoyed over the past 16 years. The other mansion in the area is Beech Hill, the history of which is describd earlier.

Much of Britain's countryside has changed dramatically since the Second World War and our 11 square miles of rural landscape has not entirely escaped this fate. In 1996 ecologist Mike Tyler, together with a group of local volunteers, carried out an environmental audit surveying each parcel of land in the parish as part of an exercise to promote sustainable development in the village. Although difficult, comparisons were also made with the Tithe Map of the 1840s. Woodland had increased from 180 to 442 acres due mainly to commercial forestry, but the number of orchards had decreased considerably. Undisturbed land decreased from 1078 to 38 acres. Areas of unimproved grassland had notably increased due to modern farming practices and the use of herbicides and fertilisers thereby having an adverse affect on traditional wild-flower meadows.

Perhaps the biggest change has been in arable farming where in 1840 only 2.5 acres were recorded under the plough compared with 1400 acres today. An exception to the rule of change was that the built-up area of the parish had changed little since 1840. The field boundaries comprised mainly Devon banks that had been in existence for hundreds of years and provided a flora-rich habitat for many species of birds, insects and mammals.

Unfortunately few records of the natural history of the parish had been recorded prior to the 20th century, but there is no reason to doubt that the loss of habitat and changing agricultural practices had had a negative effect affect on the wildlife, as experienced elsewhere in Britain.

West Aish from the air during the early 1960s.

Jean Isaacs in front of the inglenook at Scotland Farm, 1936.

Chapter 8: Home Life

Home life in the Edwardian era was very different from life today, although the kitchen still tended to serve as the headquarters. It is difficult to imagine living without electricity, telephones, cars, cookers, computers, well-surfaced roads, etc., and hard to grasp the speed of, and extent to which, changes have occurred during this century. Morchard was a very different place in which to live in 1905.

In most farmhouse kitchens of the day a large fire blazed all year round for the cooking and water heating, as well as warming the room. Often the fire was above a low oven, into which coals from the fire were placed on a tray to provide heat for cooking – the oven in the side of the chimney was lit once a week for the main baking. The door was left open while the fire burnt away inside, until the oven was hot enough to turn a piece of paper brown. The fire was then raked out and all the prepared food stood ready on long pine tables. Cakes, bread, pies, the day's lunch (prunes were well suited to this method), fruit, etc. were put in the hot oven and the door closed. As the food cooked, the oven slowly cooled thereby enhancing the flavour.

Above the main fire, suspended from the chimney hooks, hung the kettle and the boiler, adjustable, according to the height of the fire and always holding hot water. A pan was used for scalding and separating the milk to bring up the cream for butter making. The butter was churned by hand twice a week.

A few houses had a pump, which pumped cold water direct from the well, but for most it was a long haul carrying the buckets of water from a well, and sometimes from the other side of the village. There were no bathrooms and baths were taken in a tub placed in front of the fire. Toilets were usually housed in a shed at the bottom of the garden, where a bucket was emptied about once a week or the seat was sited over a pit, which was cleared once a year.

More often than not, families averaged six to ten children, which increased their poverty and

'His and hers' down the bottom of the garden. This photo was taken at Weeke Barton. The seat was situated over a land drain, so this could be described as one of the first 'water closets'!

A Visit to Morchard Bishop: Why the Population Decreased,
Extracts From A Report In The *Gazette* Dated 6 October 1905

The old world village of Morchard Bishop, situated about 2½ miles from Morchard Road Station, was a day or two since visited by representive of the 'Gazette' who wished to ascertain something about the statement by the Hon. J. Wallop that in 30 years the population had decreased by one half.

This statement was made at a meeting at Stanford when, as is usual at radical assemblies, there was an abundance of lamentations, but little in the shape of practical suggestion. Everyone agrees that the falling off of the agricultural population is a matter for regret. The conservatives had done their best to arrest it by facilitating the erection of improved cottages and lessening the burden on agriculture so that the industry may be followed with a greater chance of being remunerative, and enabling the farmer to offer more attractive terms to the labourer. But suggestions in favour of agriculture rarely meet with any sympathy from radical politicians, and, as we know, the strongest possible opposition was that extended to the renewal of the Agricultural Rates Bill; while again the suggestion likely to lead to a larger area of land being put under corn with its consequent increase in the demand for labour is opposed tooth and nail.

Mr Wallop asserted that the labouring population in the country was not increasing in numbers but in the intelligence and strength absolutely necessary for the maintenance of the vigour of the race.

Morchard Bishop presents a picturesque appearance. The majority of the buildings are cob. There are fairly broad streets and the fine old church tower arrests everyone's attention. Turning to the business in hand, our representative gathered from various sources the information given.

The population has largely decreased. That decrease commenced many years ago, but the falling average has been a gradual one.

Many years ago people not only followed agriculture, but clothes and lace were made in the village. Morchard Bishop was then, in the words of a resident – 'a very busy little place' – but, when the woollen work ceased – about 30 years since – Morchard commenced to lose ground. Mrs Wreford of Church Street who, by the way, is 86 years of age, and is still hale and hearty, stated in an interview, that she did weaving. The wool, she said, was brought in from South Molton, North Tawton and Exwick and was served out from a building opposite the London Inn, now occupied as a wheel-wright shop and... looms were to be found in almost every cottage. In some cottages were even as many as four looms. As previously stated, however an end came to this form of employment, and this had a most telling effect on the character of Morchard Bishop. A large number of young people took up making lace for an Exeter firm, but bye and bye this was also dropped, although there are one or two persons in the village who still continue lace making. Morchard Bishop is now to all intents and purposes purely agricultural.

Mr Wallop was a little out in his figures. The population at the last census which was in 1901 was 987, at the census of 1891, 102 while in the year 1851 the residents numbered 1,854. At this time, only 41 were entitled to vote.

On the whole farmers and others in and near Morchard Bishop seem to be doing fairly well in a quiet way. But the village is not what it used to be, and this fact seems to lie hard on the minds of the old people. The suspension of the woollen industry has been cited as responsible for some of the decline. But another cause was put forward. Morchard Bishop is principally comprised of glebe lands. It is stated that, while many houses have, in recent years, been pulled down, land cannot be purchased by parishioners in suitable lots for new buildings. During the last 30 years 18 houses have been taken down in Church Street alone. None have been rebuilt. In several parts of the village the ruins of old cob walls indicate the site of former dwellings. It may be said that the old dwellings which had stood the storm for many years would not have paid for repair. Probably this was so. But if as our representative was informed, people were turned out of the houses mentioned in order that they might be taken down, it would seem a pity that other houses were not built and the people retained at Morchard Bishop instead of being obliged to go elsewhere for accommodation. Only one comparatively new dwelling is, as far as our representative noticed, to be seen in Morchard Bishop, and that on the main road from the Station. Of course, it may be said that if there was a demand for houses at remunerative rates they would be built, but the business of the district does not increase and the existing accommodation suffices. The general feeling was that if any stimulus could be given to the cultivation of the land – that is, if the growing of corn were remunerative – that would arrest the decrease in the population in this and other districts and, in turn, give an impetus to other industries which would employ a greater number of hands, so increase the population and add to the prosperity of the place.

Something was said about the Radical doctrine of putting the men on the land to which the reply came, "what is the use of putting a man in the middle of a field if he hasn't the capital to buy implements, manure, seed, and stock, and cannot find the money to erect a cottage for himself?" Will Mr Wallop or Mr Lambert provide these things? If not, a man would not feel very grateful to them for sticking him up in a field with little else but a shirt and trousers, and telling him to shift for himself.

although the farmers experienced a very difficult time, the workers suffered even more. At the turn of the century the average worker's pay was 7 shillings a week (35p by today's standards).

Monday was washday when the fire would be lit under the copper in the washhouse and after the clothes had been boiled thoroughly, they were put through the large wooden mangle, before being hung on the line to dry.

Children as young as seven or eight were expected to help with the household chores and often started full-time employment after their 12th birthday. Young children, often as young as five, were expected to walk from outlying areas such as Scotland and Hare Street Farms, the three or four miles to Morchard school.

Families provided most of their own vegetables and fruit and usually kept chickens and pigs. It was a golden rule that the pigs could only be slaughtered when there was an 'r' in the month. The main joints of meat were salted down and hung up for use later. Most of the inside of the animal, including the head, was cooked and used. The wild rabbit was the staple diet of the less well off and also provided an additional income.

During the 1920s and 30s villagers would take their Sunday roast over to the two bakers for their joints to be cooked in the large ovens, at a cost of 2d. (1p) and 70 per cent of the meals would have been rabbit. The late Mrs Rice who brought up 12 children in Morchard in the hungry years said:

Rabbits was the main thing, lovely food, let me tell you, they were beautiful... Rabbits was the poor man's food, was sent by God I always think... I have cooked rabbit whole – I could skin a rabbit with anyone – and stuffed them... put them on a dish of potatoes and baked 'en... The rabbit stew, that was lovely and even the young rabbits you could fry. The harvest rabbit was the tastiest of 'em all – lovely.

The village was almost self-sufficient in food and many other necessities of life. In the 30s there were at least 20 shops, a bank and even an undertaker. Joe Burrow, who was born in 1910 recalls:

I remember one particular family called Cann, who had six children, four boys and two girls, who each year would be paraded at Burrow's the Tailors (where the present Post Office stands) to be measured for a set of corduroy clothes. They would then go to Horwells, the bootmaker's opposite, where they would all be measured for hobnailed boots. Although there were dressmakers and drapers in the village, most linen items and socks were made by the mothers and wives. Both of us boys learned tailoring. We had five people all making clothes and there was another tailor called Southcott who lived in the first house of the long thatch. We made trousers, coats and skirts, there was no ready-made clothing till 1928. Ladies made their own clothes, such as dresses.

Morchard Fair was always the second week in September which was a holiday. My family firm of tailors always put on a big meal, joint of beef and ham, and all the farmers from the outlying farmers used to come and pay their annual bills for tailoring and have a damn good feast.

Photo of Liz Brewer's sitting room, which was taken in 1915 by J.W. Perrett, who was evacuated from London to escape the Zeppelin bombing.

Memories of Morchard Bishop
by Winifred Phillips

Winifred lived in Morchard all her life (1883-1966). Her family were shopkeepers, firstly in the shop at Middle-the-Green then later at the shop in Fore Street.

The village of 'Bishop Morchard' (now known as Morchard Bishop) is situated about midway between the two great moors of Devonshire, Dartmoor and Exmoor. Before the days of motor transport it was a typical country village, the headquarters of the farming community and all that went therewith in those calm times.

The writer of this story beginning let me now mention is not old enough to remember all the many and varied occupations that went on in this village [since 1800]. But from our parents and grandparents we heard the history from time to time. The writer of this story is the last child of a family of ten children, so from hearsay she will endeavour to relate the earlier activities that was carried on in this village.

Firstly commencing with the work for the women folk, nearly every housewife helped to raise the weekly income by knitting. The yarn or wool was brought into the parish each week at a particular house on a certain day. This was then distributed to the housewife and the stockings were to be knitted by hand, and to be returned the following week. I am afraid I cannot tell you how much they got for each pair of hose, but it must have been a help to their weekly budget, more especially to the wives of farm workers whose wage at this time was small. The highest pay for the men about this time I think would have been about 7s. per week.

Housewives of today, imagine this rate of pay, for beside this their families more often averaged from eight to twelve and sometimes fourteen in numbers. How they managed to survive at all one wonders!

The farm worker was allowed a turnip and could set a trap for a rabbit occasionally if he so desired. One would hope this must happen pretty often as it must be the only time the folk ever had any kind of meat on their dinner table. The rule too was for the farm worker to be allowed a certain amount of land on the farm to plant potatoes for themselves and family. I should have stated earlier here that nearly all the cottages in this old village were built of cob and with thatched roofs, most substantial walls (in most cases) many perhaps 14 inches thick. Most have well stood the test of time far better than the modern cottages that are being built at the present time. On the right side of this old village 14 of these cob and thatch cottages were together in on block and nearing the bottom of this block of cottages and at the back was a large cob linhay that we children were told was called the 'Old Malt House'.

Later this old linhay was used for the making of Tallow candles – there were no wax candles then and these made of tallow and cotton (this was in the candle for the wick to burn). I understand that the wicks were dipped into mutton fat and hung over barrels until they dried then these candles were strung up into bundles of eight and twelve in number and sold mostly to the farmer or cattle owners who had the lanterns to carry around (these old lanterns were made of tin fitted all round with horn to be unbreakable). The inner part of these old lanterns had the bottom fitted with holders to stand the tallow candle in for safety. The horn covering did not allow much light to be shown but the old tallow wick had to be firm for use in the shippens, where there must be hay and straw for their cattle. The mutton fat used in the making of these candles was anything but a pleasant smell, however it created an industry for quite a few men folk in bygone days.

The next industry was the making of Honiton

lace and by quite a few old ladies, widows, spinsters – the writer of these pages can well remember many of these and have watched their handiwork, most beautifully done. But the time taken to the making of this lace could not have been but very little help towards their being able to keep body and soul together. The dear old ladies that I used often to visit... I feel sure their sole income was what was then known as 'Parish Pay'; this was fetched from an old butchers shop every Wednesday morning in which sat the Relieving Officer. I have heard say the amount paid out was small, but I never heard of the dear soul moaning about her amount of pay. And how they kept warm; it was rare one saw a stick of wood or coal in their open fireplaces. I think they gathered a few bits of dry wood from the coppice during the summer. I sincerely hope they did get some as their money could not be used to buy firewood or coal.

There was very little excitement in those days. The one specially big day of the year was Whit Tuesday, when the London Inn Club had their Club Walk headed by the village band – yes we had a band and they wore uniforms too, navy with gold braid and a decent number of players too.

On this particular morning, Whit Tuesday at 10 o' clock, the village band headed the procession, followed by the club members, several parishioners and children marched to the Rectory to call the Rector to march with them to the church for a special service. When service was over the band and parson, members of the club, friends and more and more, joining up on the way headed for the green where, after a few musical selections... the band dispersed for a while and the club members headed for the inn, where they always joined in a dinner followed by their usual annual club business for the past year. Many of the members wives and relatives had by this time come into the village to meet their friends while the village band gave selections during the afternoon. Three old ladies who made fairings, home-made sweets and gingerbreads, always had two stalls where there was good business done during the remainder of the day with the 'wares'. The next two or three big days was the annual 'Cattle Fair' which called for the various amusements that came from afar to brighten up the parents and children with the swings, roundabouts, shows, etc. etc. Then again out came the two 'sweet standings' who did a big business for the three days to end up the fair.

The second day of the annual fair (commencing with the sale of cattle) was followed by some horse racing, races run by men and boys – prizes given of course. This was again to be a time to meet up with their families and to join later in the evening at the usual field in which the usual pleasant fair was held. Another usual occasion was for most of the farmers and farm workers to settle up their annual bills for tailors, butchers, etc. These business folk (especially the tailors) were expected to provide a hot dinner and beer for their customers, even after waiting a year for their payments – rather a bad custom to have started but this went on for many a year. What was the usual thing too was for father to finish up at the village inn and after a few beers to call at the old friends at sweet stalls to take home a bit of 'fairing' for mother and the kids – about the only excitement they had for the year of course as there were no cars or buses then to have a day at the seaside as happens nowadays. As one grows older one thinks and wishes their lives and those of their families could have had a little more life and change but I suppose it was really impossible at this particular period of their lives.

I am thinking now in particular of the dear old souls who tried very hard to eke out a livelihood by doing the lovely 'lace work'. I feel sure they could earn very little by working this beautiful lace. It was very fine work and most trying for their eyes, one of the old ladies that I used to visit had to wear two pairs of spectacles to see the cotton that she was using. As a young child I was most amused and interested – she was a jolly little lady and full of fun, her son used to be working in the little kitchen with her, this work was repairs to suits for men folk. Another lace worker was a sweet little soul that lived near our village school and who must have been kept from her lace work

THE BOOK OF MORCHARD BISHOP

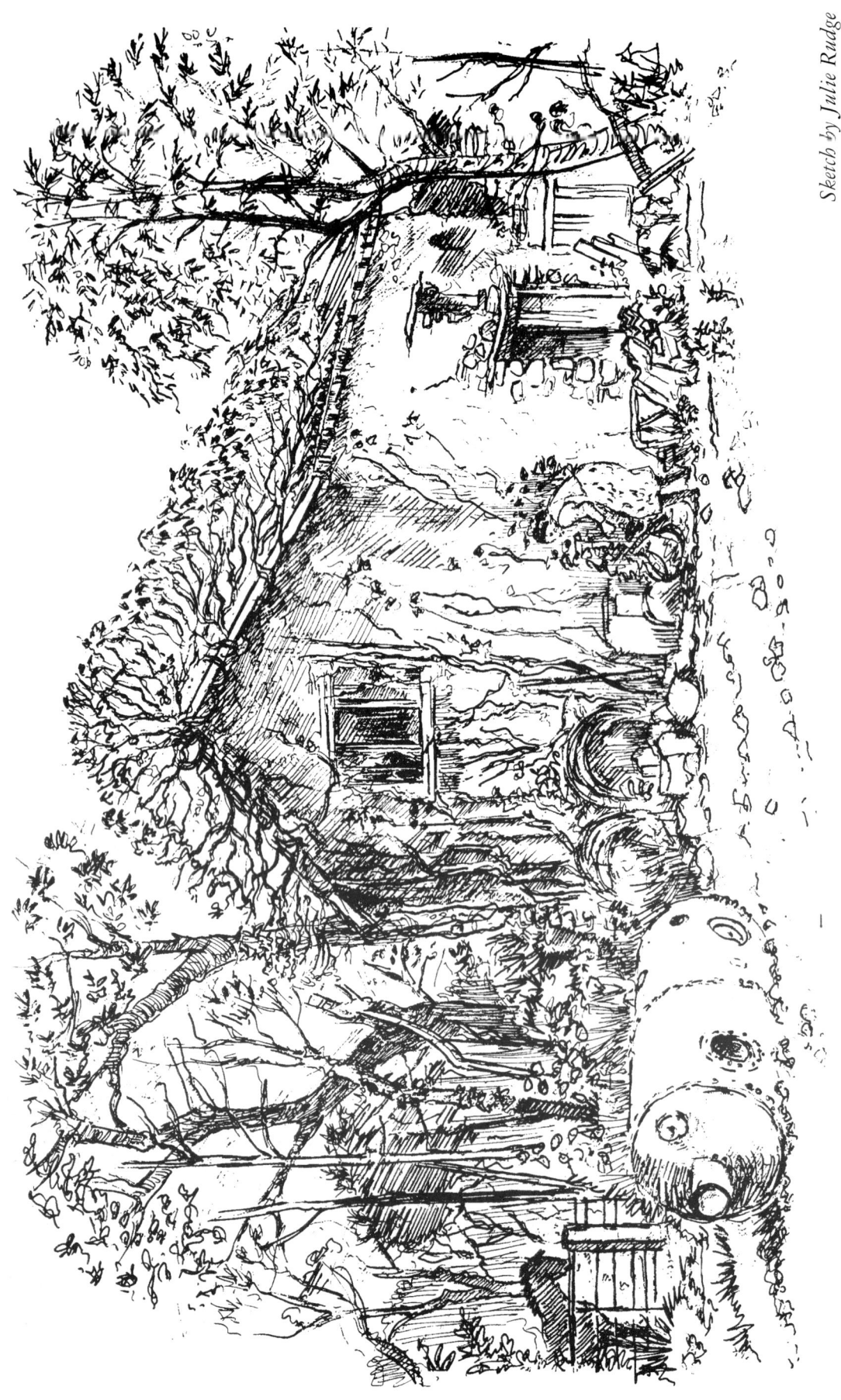

Sketch by Julie Rudge

A charitable trust spent £800 putting a mobile home for Liz Brewer and providing bedding but she still refused to move in, insisting that the new home was not for her but for her neighbours. Eventually neighbours managed to convince this semi-recluse that she should leave the cottage in which she was born (see opposite below) and move into the mobile home, where she lived happily for a number of years before she died in the late 1990s.

many hours during the week by we kiddies calling at her door for a cup of water. I think she must have fetched quite a little distance from her cottage too, for she had a large bath filled every day from which she dipped a clean cup for a drink when we called. There were I think about 200 children, perhaps more, attending the school and never once was a child refused a drink. I believe it was more to see her smile and kindly manner that made us children knock on her door ... We never realised what a hindrance it must have been for the dear soul. My mother was always telling me not to worry her... and I feel sure that if anyone has gone to heaven it will be 'Aunt Fanny' as we all knew her.

She lived in a little cottage quite near the church and never once did she miss a service, be it on Sunday or week day always in her little black cloak and black close-fitting bonnet. When she passed on, the school children all followed her coffin and later had a stone cross erected to her memory – no one ever filled her place; after she left us children the cup of cold water came from the pump in the school yard.

The village school is just across the main road from our parish church, which is a very nice size one and nicely kept up. In it is a lovely screen, an unusual lovely design [which] was restored some years ago by the kindness of the late Hon. John Wallop who resided there at the Portsmouth's family... Barton House. After his lordship's decease, his brother and his wife, who came from Wyoming, came to Barton House to reside. They of course were Lord and Lady Portsmouth. I need hardly say these were both most popular and were welcomed by the whole parish. Their kindness and pleasant manner endeared them to the rich and poor alike. After the death of Lady Portsmouth the Earl left our parish here, to live with his son at the family seat in Hampshire. This son who takes the name of Lord Lymington is living now with his family there. (I should have mentioned that our Earl Portsmouth did not live but a short time after his wife's decease.)

Liz Brewer's cottage in Oldborough which became derelict to such an extent that in the late 1970s it was necessary to demolish part of it to prevent it falling into the road. The other part of this cob cottage soon fell into disrepair, the roof bowed and some of the cob walls collapsed. Even though she was liable to be buried alive, she still continued to live there, much to the concern of many caring neighbours, and the Parish and District Councils.

WATER

The Parish Council minute book records numerous entries relating to water problems in the village, particularly in dry weather. The problem became so acute in the late 1920s, that the Minister of Health, Neville Chamberlain (*right*) visited the village to inspect the wells.

In 1935 the Crediton Rural District Council approved the drilling of a bore hole on the land behind the council houses in Church Street, and in spite of the hole being sunk to 450 feet, the scheme was abandoned, due to lack of water, in April 1938. A huge tank had been erected opposite the school and water pipes had been laid in the roads. In May 1938 a new well was constructed near Wood Lane and this was connected to the new reservoir but still the water supply was not plentiful.

In March 1948 the water shortage was very serious and had, by this time, become the responsibility of the North Devon Water Board. They decided to pipe the water from Bugford Quarry to the village reservoir and George Burrow was employed to drive an 800 gallon tanker, carrying water at least once a week from Bugford to the village. He was instructed to add two small chlorine tablets to each load and, if he wasn't sure whether he had put the tablets in, was advised to put in some more.

In 1953 the Dartmoor supply reached Morchard Bishop, the standpipes were removed and the village enjoyed an internal water supply. Water pressure was still a problem until the late 1980s, when a new supply pipe was brought in from Lapford.

Villagers often had to carry water from the other side of Morchard to their homes.

REFUSE

It was not until 1925 that the first refuse collection took place and that initially was once every three months but was later extended, in 1927, to every month. Jim Ford, who then owned Crockers, collected the rubbish on his horse and cart and buried this in a pit in his garden. For collecting the rubbish and keeping the village clean, he was paid the grand sum of £4 per year by the Parish Council. In 1941 he got a pay rise of £2 p.a. and was paid £16 p.a. by the Crediton Rural District for collecting the refuse from Morchard and Lapford.

Electricity

Most Devon towns had coal gas from the 1800s, and in 1888 Okehampton was the first Devon town to have a public supply of electricity, produced by water turbine, shortly followed by Exeter's coal-fired, steam-powered station in New North Road. In the 1930s main generating stations were linked by the construction of the 132kv grid system, bringing large, overhead pylons striding over Devon.

In June 1931, the Parish Council appealed to the Crediton RDC to ask the Exe Valley Electricity Co. to include the parish in its scheme. It was not until March 1936 that the company agreed to an extension of an electricity supply at Lapford. In early 1937, the village finally enjoyed electricity, although some outlying farms were not connected until 1964.

If a house only had four lights they were installed free and cost 1 shilling (5p) a week to run. Apparently, if householders turned on more than two lights at a time the power failed.

Florrie Mildon moved into No. 3 Whites Cottages on the day she married in March 1938 and recalls:

We had no mod cons. There was a toilet at the end of the garden which we shared with two other families. There was mains water but not in the cottages; we shared a pump.

The three cottages were rented and the other two families had indoor water and toilets put in, but I hadn't room for a toilet.

I had a black lead stove for cooking and had to bring water in, boil it on top of the stove for washing, then take it back outside as we had no indoor sink. When Mr Waller took over as landlord he put in the cold water tap inside for me.

There was electricity installed when we moved in, but we didn't have it connected. Eventually we got it put on and I got a washing boiler and, in time, a fridge and cooker. I never had running hot water there. I still used the outside toilet until I moved to the old peoples' bungalows opposite the Memorial Hall in March 1993, six months after my husband Bill died.

The Morchard Bishop Cook Book

In 1988 the *Cook Book* was devised and compiled by Pam Cox, Jill Greig, Liz Hall, Alison Orchard, Lyn Padley, Julie Page, John Smith and Teresa Tyldesley on behalf of the Morchard Bishop School Association and in aid of school funds. Over 500 copies were sold and unfortunately the book is no longer available. People who lived or worked in the village donated this collection of traditional and favourite recipes. Here is an extract from the book:

When I was a schoolgirl we used to sing this song to fill out the afternoon on a Friday:

Squab Pie, Junket and cider brew,
Richest of cream from the cow
What 'ud old England without them do,
And where would they be to now?
As crumpy as a lump of bread,
Be a loaf without good leaven,
And the yeast Mother England do use for her bread,
Be Devon, Glorious Devon!

Where I lived when I was 14 was a farm called Duckham near Chawleigh. The mistress, Miss Winnie, made a squab pie and her brother came in and thought it smelt so good that he decided he couldn't wait till tea time and, thinking it was apple pie he got out the bowl and put a big dollop of cream on top. As soon as he tasted the onions he knew what he'd done but he had it just the same. I can picture farmer John's face now, it's like it's yesterday in my mind.

Pastry
Leftover cooked pork or lamb (cut into small pieces)
Sliced onion
Sliced cooking apple
Pinch of salt

Line a plate with half the pastry. Mix the pork, onion, apple and salt and pile the mixture into the plate. Cover the pastry top and cook for half an hour at Gas Mark 5, (180°C/ 375°F) until the top is brown and the vegetables are cooked. If you leave a slit in the top to let the steam out then you can test if the onion and apple are cooked using a skewer.

Florrie Mildon

THE BOOK OF MORCHARD BISHOP

Six sets of twins in one village (photo taken c.1977) – how many communities of the size of Morchard can boast that?
The recent arrival of twin sons for the Rev. Reynolds, Rector of Morchard Bishop, brought the number of sets of twins to six. Five out of the six were baptised in the parish, four are in the Sunday School.
(Left to right) back row: Rachel and Louise Wimberley held by Mrs Hooper and Mrs Wimberley; Andrew and Philip Donovan with their mother; Richard and Christopher Reynolds, held by Mrs Reynolds and Mrs Glover;.
front row: Jenny and Sarah Hill with their mother; Georgina and Melanie Rice with their mother; Philip and Michael Cousins with their mother.
(Mrs Glover is also a twin and her sister, Mrs Ada Hooper, had twin daughters).

Everyday Morchard Memories

"Men used to come and have their haircut in the blacksmith shop, sometimes they sat on the anvil. On Sunday mornings they would come in for a haircut and then they used to go up to 'Maunders Linhay' opposite 'Paradise' where a farmer kept his cider. I think they only used the haircut as an excuse to get drunk."

"The Band used to go around the village playing at Christmas and used to finish up at West Aish or Oxen Park and they would be drunk by the time they got there. They had lots of home-made cider on the way".

"There was a grey stone in the churchyard and the light from Ridge House used to reflect on it. They used to say if you walked around the stone seven times you will hear the angels sing. One evening, I was in the school gardens with the schoolmaster's son, Vernon Tipper, when some people went up to this gravestone and they walked around the stone seven times. They didn't know we were there. We started to sing. They were so shocked one of them fainted".

"If you were ill, Doctor Pratt would give you a bottle of pink medicine. We used to call it 'Pratt's Popular Paint'.

"Opposite the beginning of the long row of thatched cottages used to be a baker called Fred Way. One day he got drunk and hung his wife's bloomers out of the window. They were full of dough".

Violet Buckingham was born in 1912 and spent the latter part of her life at Fountain Head:

"I did some sewing and dressmaking at home after the First World War. Then Lady Portsmouth came to me, offering me a job as her personal maid. I was very good at sewing and dressmaking and used to make jumpers and blouses for her and also all her underwear. I travelled all over Britain with her. I earned 25s. a week and lived in. I had no time off as I was always on call. When I did have a holiday I came home to the family."

Morchard Today

If Morchard was a poverty-stricken parish at the turn of the century and by the middle of the decade life had improved very considerably, what do the residents thinks of it as the millennium looms into view? The local 'Agenda 21' group carried out a Village Appraisal in 1995 and, as over half of the parishioners responded to the questionnaire, we have a fairly accurate picture. Most people were very happy living in Morchard, with just under half 'wanting it to stay as it is' and approximately 40 per cent 'wanting to see it develop as a working community'.

Some 6 per cent had lived in the parish for less than 16 years and only 27 per cent had resided there for more than 26 years, the new arrivals coming from all age groups.

Of those who gave their occupational details, 39 per cent worked in administration, local government and professional occupations, and only 20 per cent in agriculture.

Over two-thirds travelled, studied or worked outside the parish, with 41 per cent commuting ten or more miles a day.

The overwhelming view is that most people are happy living in this popular village and, as they say, "It is just lovely as it is!"

Fore Street tradesmen, 1897 (left to right) standing: Chas. Smith (blacksmith), Mr Howard, Tom Conibeer (saddlemaker), Alfred Philips, Ned Way (baker), Tom Smith (blacksmith); sitting: unknown, Jack Brownson, Walter Horwill, George Burrow (tailor), W. Southcott, (tailor), Will Burrow (tailor).

Chapter 9: Occupations, Trade and Commerce

At the turn of the century the village had as many as 30 shops doing business at one time. Some weaving and lace making took place, but with agriculture being by far the biggest local industry, most of the small concerns were connected with farming in one way or another.

Above and below: Morchard tradespeople, 1999
(Left to right) back: Chris Hutchings and Pat Rice (builders), Andy Rice (plumber), Richard Frost (thatcher), Richard Tapp (builder);
front: Harold and Mervin Webber (blacksmiths), Dick Frost (thatcher), Brian Wilshaw (heating engineer), Michael Tapp (carpenter).

(Left to right) standing: Duncan Howes (milkman), Steve Carter (Post Office), Terry Butler (hairdresser), Roger Brooking (Post Office), Nick Gurr (Car Care Garage), Peter Miles and John Snell (Polson Hill Garage), Norman Rice (butcher);
seated: Janice Butler (hairdresser), Yvonne Rice (grocer), Vera and Sarah Gillbard (London Inn).

Morchard Trades Through the Years

Above: The Old Candle Factory– demolished in the 1980s. This building was also used at one time as a distribution centre for wool which arrived in the village from South Molton, North Tawton and Exwick. The wool was then worked on the numerous looms around the area.
Above right: Les Rice, the oldest of 12 Rice children, has been the regular village gravedigger for over 40 years.
Below: Miss Palfrey's draper's shop in the 1940s.

Left: Albert Pugsley's grocer's shop at the Fountain Head, Polson Hill, December 1920.

Above: Miss Bennett's sweet shop, 1910.

Left: Margaret Philips outside her grocer's shop in 1920 (which closed in the 1950s). On the left are Gladys and Aileen Chanter. Note the unmade road with the potholes.

Morchard Trades Through the Years

Left: Polson garage before it was rebuilt in 1988. It was once the premises of Drew Brothers (below and bottom), who were well-known agricultural engineers.

Oldborough Quarry

Stone had been extracted from this quarry for possibly 200 years, but in the early 1950s A. Nott and Sons started to rent it and they became one of the major employers in the area. At it's peak it employed 32 men, and provided stone for repairing roads in the area. At that time a quarry labourer could expect to be paid £5 for a 40-hour week, which was £2 more than a farm labourer. In 1971 the owner of the quarry, Bill Brewer of Lower Oldborough, was concerned that the quarrying was endangering the stability of his house, as the blasting was getting nearer and he terminated the contract.

Today this is a fishing retreat providing peaceful entertainment to hundreds of fishermen every year.

Right: Oldborough Quarry showing office and Weighbridge just inside the gate.

Below: Photo taken by the Clerk, Charlie Morgan. Left to right: Fred Stentiford, H. Oaylen, A. Ridd, Bert Brimilcombe, J. Burak, R. Doe, R. Wyatt. (M. Edwards is in the rear of the photo.).

Blacksmithing in Morchard

Right: Charles Smith outside his blacksmith shop between the wars at Middle-the-Green.

Far left, left and below: Mervin and Harold Webber are at least the third generation of blacksmiths to work in this workshop. It is thought that their grandfather started the business but it may be older. With the exception of some modern equipment, work still continues in the traditional manner.

The Village Thatcher

The village thatcher, Richard Frost, is at least the 5th generation to run the family business. He took over from his father, Dick, when he retired in the late 1980s.

Although water reed is sometimes used, Richard and his father have always used the traditional locally-grown wheat straw, which has to be cut with a binder and stacked in stooks. This is stored in stacks and then combed in the traditional way during the winter months.

The Frosts thatched the house in the photograph below, Woodparks, 27 years ago which was, at that time, an average life for a thatched roof (as opposed to only 15 years today – it is thought that modern farming methods affect the length of the straw's life). It appears that thatching is just as popular as ever and more men are taking up the trade. Normally when a roof is re-thatched new straw replaces the old but sometimes new rafters are required as well, making the job even more involved than it is normally.

Today's Ventures

Some new small industries have grown up in the area, usually employing one or two people – most prominent of these is the worlds biggest single industry, tourism. There are almost ten houses that provide bed and breakfast, most of their trade coming from walkers on the Two Moors Way and four more which provide self-catering accommodation. Perhaps it is not surprising that the Post Office is also a Tourist Information Centre. This is run in conjunction with the District Council and the Devonshire Heartland Tourism Association.

Professional and semi-professional people, who are able to work from home using the latest information technology, now occupy several of the larger houses.

A. E. Partridge and Sons started their Livestock Haulage business in the village in 1946, and have continued to operate road haulage ever since. In 1996 they outgrew The Laurels and moved the majority of their vehicles to Exeter.

The business that was started by Archie and Mabel Partridge continued to grow under the supervision of their sons Brian and Keith and their grandsons, Alan and Michael, are now the driving force.

Cottage Gardens (*below and bottom*) was started in 1990 by partners Roger Holloway and David McKie on a two-and-a-half acre site where they grow perennials which they supply to garden centres all over the South West. The business has now expanded and employs five local people.

COTTAGE GARDENS
HERBACEOUS PERENNIALS
UPCOTT NURSERY
UPCOTT, MORCHARD BISHOP
CREDITON, DEVON EX17 6NG
TEL: 01363 877258
FAX: 01363 877557

Chapter 10: Serving the Parish

Where would societies be without those individuals who, whether paid or unpaid, perform those tasks so often taken for granted? Whether in the smallest village or our larger cities, it is the unsung heroes – parish councillors, policemen, club secretaries and doctors, to name but a few – that contribute so much to the lifeblood of the community, despite being often taken for granted and even criticised when they strive to do their very best.

As far as our parish is concerned I can think of no better example than George Burrow who, by the time of his retirement as Clerk to the Morchard Bishop Parish Council in April 1990, had served in that capacity for 53 years, having missed only three meetings – surely a national record!

It is interesting to note that his predecessor William 'Ginger' Leach served in that capacity from 1894 until handing over to George in 1937. The third parish clerk was Pauline Nott who continued until Mary Bourne was appointed in 1992. George, who himself was a good cricketer and footballer, was very much at the centre of the Playing Field Association, until he died in 1998.

Three other great individuals who were so highly respected and did so much for the Parish were of course Lord Portsmouth, Doctor Pratt (the village doctor) and David Tipper (the village schoolmaster) and their wives, who played an important part in the building of the Memorial Hall. It appears from earlier literature that Lord Portsmouth was affectionately known as 'father'.

George Burrow (courtesy of the Crediton Courier*).*

Much of their voluntary work was also directed towards improving the health and wellbeing of a community that had suffered, and was still suffering from, difficult times. Another important organisation they set up was the Morchard Bishop and District Nursing Association, which did much to improve health facilities in the area before the National Health Service was set up in 1948.

Lord Portsmouth and David Tipper with the village band, c.1931.

The village schoolmaster, David Tipper MBE, with a group of his pupils, 1920s.

Nurse Pope born at 'Crockers'. She later became the district nurse and midwife from 1928-48.

Members of the Morchard Bishop Special Constabulary.
(Left to right) back row: E. Gunn, P. Colton, Jim Luggar, Henry Dockings, R. Wright, Percy Dockings; front row: Sgt unknown, Tom Oatway, unknown, Harry Dockings.

The Village Band around the turn of the century.
Included in the photo are Ernest Delve (far left, standing), Charles Howard (third from the left, standing), bandmaster Frank Howard (third from the left, seated) and Herbert Howard (far right, seated).

Ernest Bevin
The Country Boy

As we approach the end of the 20th century, historians will be debating who were the great British politicians and reformers of the century, and no doubt among the list will be Lloyd George, Winston Churchill, and of course Margaret Thatcher. At the very top should undoubtedly be Ernest Bevin. A man who excelled as an orator and leader of men, founder of the Transport and General Workers Union, Minister of Labour and National Service in Winston Churchills wartime cabinet, and also the post-war Foreign Secretary.

Prior to his sudden death in April 1951, he could have claimed some credit for setting up Wages Councils, the Welfare State and the Marshall Plan (which helped a bankrupt Europe recover after the war). Possibly his greatest achievements were the Berlin Airlift of 1948 and his part in the founding of NATO which has arguably provided us with 50 years of peace; but is unlikely that Mr Bevin would have voiced his successes. He was a modest man who declined knighthoods and titles on many occasions. The only honour he received was on his death; his ashes were placed in the national shrine – Westminister Abbey.

He disliked fuss. He liked things kept simple and practical. No doubt his childhood would have considerably influenced his personality and attitude to life. Whilst most of his contemporary politicians attended Eton, Harrow, Cambridge or Oxford, Ernest's educational record reads: Winsford, Morchard Bishop, Colbrooke and Haywards Schools. At the age of 11 his full-time education had finished and he became a farmboy on two different farms at Copplestone, Devon, and later a labourer in Bristol.

Diana Mercy Bevin was 40 years old on 7 March 1881, when she gave birth to her sixth son and seventh child, Ernest, at the small village of Winsford, Somerset. Since 1877 she had described herself as a widow, working as a domestic help in farms, in homes, the 'Royal Oak' inn, and also acted as the village midwife. She undertook every job she could find to feed her young, hungry family. They were described as the poorest family in the village. Her only consolation was her burning faith. She was a staunch Nonconformist and every Sunday she took her family to the tin chapel in the village and even though Ernest was illegitimate (she refused to name his father) she still treasured her son and treated him no differently from her other six children. When Ernest was just eight years old his mother died.

The plaque erected in honour of Ernest Bevin at Morchard School.

It was his half sister, Mary Pope, and her husband George who brought this orphan the 30 miles to Shobrooke Farm in Morchard Bishop. Although George worked as a railwayman at Morchard Road Station and probably saw the new, standard gauge railway track introduced on that railway line in 1892, his family had been tenant farmers since before 1840 at nearby Nathorne farm and continued farming at Shobrooke until 1923 when its present owners, Mr and Mrs Shapland bought it in 1923.

The school log at Morchard Bishop School shows he commenced there on the 20 May 1889, three weeks after his mother's death. It had just two classrooms in those days, one for the boys and one for the girls.

In the following autumn he moved with his foster parents to a cob and thatched cottage called 'Tiddly-Winks' in Copplestone, which is now opposite the mill on the A377 road.

In spite of the poverty of the time, the Popes took good care of their charge for three years but expected him to work hard at home. In Alan Bullocks book *The Life and Times of Ernest Bevin*, the local postman describes how he often saw young Ernest in the early hours of the morning getting water from two streams which ran across the hilly fields opposite, cascading into the ditch adjacent to the main Barnstaple Road. Those were the days before pumps were fitted outside houses. Apparently, like so many children of the times, he suffered from terrible chilblains on his hands.

Another chore which was expected of him before leaving for school, was peeling potatoes and cleaning boots. Mark Steven mentions in his book *Ernest Bevin*, that in 1944, when stationed with Winston Churchill in a special train at Droxford to watch the troops prepare for the invasion of

Normandy, Churchill discovered that the Minister of Labour and National Service – as Bevin then was – cleaned his own boots. Horrified that the man responsible for mobilising the entire country had to look after himself, Churchill gave instructions for Bevin to have a batman. Bevin was not keen. 'I wouldn't like you to do that, Prime Minister,' he said, 'I get such splendid ideas when I'm cleaning my boots'. Molotov the Soviet Foreign Secretary was also horrified when he found Bevin cleaning his own boots.

As there was no school in Copplestone in 1889 he walked the two miles to the old two-classroomed school at Colbrooke which is situated just north of the village and today is just a roofless ruin. Apparently the schoolmaster, Mr Sharland, helped him very considerably with his reading.

Encouraged by his foster parents, Ernest regularly attended the Copplestone 'Ebenezer' chapel which had been opened the previous year, and like his mother, he remained a staunch Nonconformist until he died. The term 'Ebenezer' is taken from the old testament (1 Samuel; chapter 7; verse 12) and means the 'stone of help' which was very appropriate for that deprived orphan. Today the chapel is a thriving community in the very centre of village life.

Mrs Pope managed to secure a place in Haywards Boys School in Crediton where he commenced on 2 September 1890. Ernest reached Standard W in July 1891 and not only was he entitled to receive a 'Labour Certificate', he was also allowed to leave school although he remained there until 25 March 1892.

One interesting story was told some years ago by Dame Georgina Buller, daughter of General Buller: in connection with some charity work she went to see Ernest Bevin whilst he was Minister of Labour but on arrival found his waiting room full of people queuing to see him. She had hardly arrived before her name was called and she was ushered into the Minister's room. She was so surprised that she had been invited to jump the queue and asked the Minister why she had received preferential treatment. He replied 'I wanted to see what you looked like when I heard that you had arrived. As a boy I went to school at Haywards and was caught stealing apples from your father's orchard at Downes, Crediton and was given a good hiding'.

The Dame congratulated him adding 'And look where it got you. You are a Minister'. The interview lasted some time as the great man talked of Crediton.

At the age of 11 years and 16 days Ernest completed his formal education and he became a farmboy living in at Chaffcombe Farm earning 6d. a week for a ten-hour day, six days a week, which was payable on quarter days. His duties included herding the cows, scaring birds, picking up stones, and cutting mangolds and turnips for cattle. In the evening he would read the *Bristol Mercury* newspaper to his employers in front of the fire.

He commenced his new job in the winter of 1892/3 with farmer William Snell May where he managed to double his wages and earn 1 shilling per week. His career as a farm boy came to an abrupt end in the 1894 after a disagreement with farmer May about the amount of cattle food he had chopped up one morning. Villagers in Copplestone claim that the farmer hid himself in a cupboard to avoid the irate 13-year-old who had armed himself with a bill hook. Beer farm is still a working farm today and is owned by Farmer May's grandson, Michael.

Ernest's brother Jack had written urging him to join his other five brothers in Bristol and seek his fortune there, so it was not surprising that he decided that country life was not for him and joined the hundreds of thousands of poor villagers who had fled to the town since 1870, taking the train from the tiny Copplestone railway station to what was then Britain's second largest city, and thriving port, Bristol.

Above: Recycling Group (left to right): Julie Rudge, Sonja Andrews, Ken Orchard, Claire Poiretti, Sarah Robinson, Freda Wicks.

Small Recycling Initiative Beats Whitehall Targets

A Devon village is leading the way in waste recycling. Morchard Bishop has become the first community in the country to reach the Government's 25 per cent target for recycling of household rubbish.

The scheme was set up in 1989, then becoming only the second weekly multi-material collection in the country. However many other communities throughout the country have followed the successful Morchard formula.

Founder member, Julie Page said the group was surprised by its success. 'It seems a long time ago that we started our little project and we certainly never expected it to grow into a major scheme with the kind of influence it has throughout the country. We now get enquiries and requests for advice from all over the UK and occasionally from abroad, particularly the former Communist block.'

The group comprises about 25 local volunteers who have proved that the recycling can be financially viable. It now donates at least £1,000 annually to other projects in the parish.

(Courtesy of Express and Echo, *1 March 1994)*

"THE MORCHARD MESSENGER"

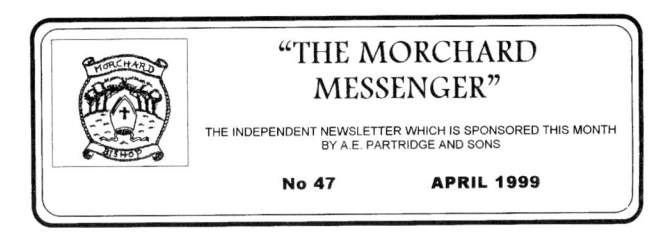

THE INDEPENDENT NEWSLETTER WHICH IS SPONSORED THIS MONTH BY A.E. PARTRIDGE AND SONS

No 47   **APRIL 1999**

In 1995 following the successful VE Souvenir Programme and Village Directory, the Morchard Messenger came into being. This is an independent, free monthly newsletter distributed to most of the 400 households in the community. Although normally only A4 size, it keeps everyone in the village informed of activities and news.

Its success can be measured by its co-operation. There are always plenty of organisations, firms and individuals who are prepared to pay the £45 needed each month to sponsor it and plenty of copy left at the Post Office each month to fill the pages. The energetic Mrs Howard distributes it to all the houses in the village, and copies are available in the shops and garage, for those who live further away. There is even a postal service available.

Among the volunteers who make it possible are Mike Tyler, who provides a regular countryside article and proof reads, Janet Symons who looks after the diary dates and Mary Bourne, the treasurer. Long may it continue.

PATHWAY ASSOCIATION

Probably the oldest manmade (or womanmade!) objects in our parish are the footpaths – older than all the buildings, the roads and even the ancient hedgerows. Celtic man travelled across Devon using these paths, many of which were later made into roads.

The common law of the land protected these ancient thoroughfares and although today we have legislation that protects them, problems do occur. In 1896 our newly-formed Parish Council was keen to preserve the footpaths when our rector the Rev. J.C. Blackmore 'Caused an obstruction to be erected in the Footpath (now No. 13 near Frost) in Fair Downs'. A motion was carried that 'Members of the Parish Council shall go to Fair Down with other Parishioners and remove it'. In 1914, signatures were collected for a 'petition to be presented to the County Council' due to Mr Wallop (presumably Lord Portsmouth) 'Refusing to allow' Worlington and Morchard Bishop Councils 'To re-erect the footpath at Deneridge' (now footpath 31).

As late as 12 September 1983, 16 of our parishioners walked the lane from Weeke Barton to Middlecott Farm in protest, when the owner was trying to close it.

In 1828, before Barton House could be built, the Rev. John Comyns Churchill, husband of Lady Henrietta Churchill (daughter of Lord Portsmouth) applied for a diversion to move a footpath that ran across the site. The proposal was advertised in the paper for three weeks and Mr James Wentworth Buller and Mr J. Sillifant signed the document, which is now held in the Record Office at Exeter.

In 1952 the Parish Council left the area a wonderful heritage of 42 footpaths, totalling 20 miles – some with the most spectacular views of Dartmoor and it is not surprising that more and more visitors each year come to stay in bed and breakfast and self-catering accommodation. These walkers and tourists bring a very welcome £38 million per year to the regional economy.

Volunteers, including Bill Edmonds, erecting a stile near 'Cricket' in 1988.

In the late 1970s Joe Turner and his wife from Exeter connected a number of local footpaths across the county, to provide a long-distance footpath from Ivybridge to Exmoor, thus creating the famous 'Two Moors Way'. Annually over 1000 walkers enjoy the peace and tranquillity of our beautiful countryside. In May 1978 the Chairman of the Devon County Council, Ted Pinney, flew in by helicopter to unveil the halfway stone opposite the church and 21 years later, in 1998, the Chairman of the Mid Devon District Council, David Pugsley, demonstrated his keeness for this walk when he was joined by Nick Harvey, the local MP, Jeremy Lee, a District Councillor, Roger Holloway, the Chairman of our Parish Council, and many others, to walk the Mid-Devon section from Cheriton Bishop to Witheridge.

Our Pathway Association was formed in response to the Devon County 'Adopt-a-Footpath' scheme in 1988 and fortunately our Parish Council has always been supportive of the Association. The village was the first in Mid Devon to receive a map showing the parish footpaths, and when the District Council published their Circular Walks Leaflets, Morchard again featured in the first.

It was very encouraging when the Parish Council was one of the first to be offered participation in the nationwide Parish Paths Partnership Scheme. Under this scheme the parish receives funds from the County Council and the Countryside Commission to improve the public path network. Today our parish is used as a model for other parishes on how co-operation between landowners, walkers, volunteers, parish, district and county councils, can provide an effective network of footpaths. Much of this is due to the enthusiasm, patience and diplomacy of Julie Rudge. We hope that future generations will continue to protect and enjoy our national heritage into the 21st century and beyond.

Halfway point on the 'Two Moor Way'.

View of Dartmoor – sketch by Julie

Another unexpected visitor blocking the footpath at 'Fairdown'.

OTHER PLACES OF INTEREST

The story of the pound illustrates how our beautiful village can be improved at the same time as preserving our heritage for future generations. In 1980 Mrs Audrey Densham Tanner (née Ware) from South Africa wrote to our Gardening Club pointing out that she had recently visited her ancestral home and wanted to donate a tree to the village to commemorate her ancestors.

Various sites were considered, one of which was a large mound of earth in the centre of Broadgate lane, at the junction of Polson Hill. Devon County Council suggested the tree be planted opposite the garage, and during the tidying of the site, the remains of the pound were found and with the help of volunteers the area was greatly improved.

The ancient pound was used to impound animals found straying in the area, and the following entry is shown in the 'Jury Presentments of Morchard Bishop Memorial Court' Register:

At the 1682 Court the death of a tenant and his wife was reported, and the new tenant recorded.
THE POUND was presented as being in a ruinous and decayed state. John Philip was sworn as Reeve for the year.

The 1889 map tells us that there was an ancient monument on the triangular site at Peters Green and an article 'Ancient Stone Crosses of Devon' by E. Masson Philips (published under the Transactions of the Devonshire Association), also mentions a cross at this location. It was classed as type B-C, i.e. of the 14th century. Although the possibility of crosses marking spots where people were hanged was considered, the view was that they were actually way/crossroad markers or boundary markers between estates.

In 1957 it was reported that the stone had been damaged at some time and lay against a shed nearby.

Above: Peters Green (outside Weeke Barton).
Top: The remains of the Morchard Bishop Cross.

The Village Pound

Above: The planting of the cherry tree which led to the re-discovery of the village pound. (Left to right): George Down, Peter O'Brien, Mrs Wheeley, Sid Robert.

Left: Hilda Carta, Margaret Bell and Bert Brimilcombe restoring the pound, 1981.

Below and top: The finished pound complete with a plaque to mark the occasion.

This piece of land, which lies on a three-way junction, is known as Jane Way's Grave. It was a favourite place for tipping rubbish until restored by Antony Heale, Roger Holloway and others in the 1980's to provide an idyllic resting place to enjoy the wonderful view over Dartmoor. Nobody knows who Jane Way was but a clue to her story may lie in the ancient belief that the devil could not claim a suicide's soul if the corpse was buried at a crossroads.

Returning ex-servicemen, 1919.

Dedication of the War Memorial, 11 July 1920.

Chapter 11: The War Years

With the exception of the Civil War, Morchard had rarely been affected by the nation's conflicts until the summer of 1914. One of the first visible indications would have been seeing a dozen local farmers, who were part of the 1st Battalion of the Devonshire Yeomanry, parading outside the London Inn, dressed in their smart uniforms and mounted on their own horses, riding out of the village on their way to war. By contrast, the local farm-workers who formed part of the 5th Battalion of the Devonshire Regiment rode out of the village on their bicycles. The village war memorial records the names of the 24 men who were not to return to their love ones.

The 1914-18 war had an immense influence on the community, with many of the young men never returning home. Of those who did, still more were to suffer from the effects of wounds and gas attacks for the rest of their lives.

As the 1930s progressed, the threat of war seemed imminent once again. Hopes of 'peace in our time' finally subsided on 3 September 1939. Once again we were at war with Germany. Once again both the young men and women were being called to serve their country. This time things were different. In the first war, conscription was not introduced until 1917 and most of the men were volunteers. In the Second World War it was introduced in 1939 for the 18 to 25-year-olds and this was extended in May 1940.

The Emergency Powers Act of 1940 required all men and women between the ages of 16 and 64 to register with the Minister of Labour, who had the power 'to direct any person in the United Kingdom to perform any such service as the Minister might specify'. Not only were people directed into the armed services but also into armament factories, railways, into the coal mines, into agriculture and many other essential services. Refusal to comply could result in imprisonment.

It is interesting to note that this all-powerful Minister of Labour was none other than Ernest Bevin, the eight-year-old orphan who had come to Morchard Bishop to live with his half sister at Shobroke Farm, after his mother died (see Chapter 10: Serving the Parish).

Many measures were introduced which had an immediate effect on the community. Food, coal and petrol were rationed; gas masks had been issued. Blackout regulations, which forbade the after-dark use of a light that could be seen from the air, were introduced and enforced by the local A.R.P. (Air Raid Precautions) wardens. An auxiliary fire service was also set up in the village which was equipped with a hand cart, ladders and stirrup pumps to fight fires caused by enemy action. Long ladders and hoses were hung on the London Inn wall in Church Street.

Many children who had been evacuated from London arrived in the village and were billeted with local families, and numbers increased in June 1940 when 87 children and 4 teachers arrived from Merton and Wimbledon. Rosemary Dobson, one of the evacuees, recalls:

One of the most vivid memories in my life was boarding a train in Wimbledon with hundreds of other tearful children. I was frightened by the prospect of

Mixing with the townies (left to right) Marian and Freda Woodward (evacuees from Wimbledon) with Babs Edwards and Freda Sowden (now Mrs Heggadon).

leaving my parents and my home for an unknown destination.

Eventually the train pulled into Crediton station and a coach took us to Morchard Bishop. My friend and I went to live with a Mrs and Mrs Greenslade and their daughter, Lilian at Lane End Farm. They were very kind to us and tried to make us feel at home but everything was so different, so quiet. We had to get water from a pump or from a stream on the other side of the road. There was no electricity, only oil lamps, no streetlights and I was very afraid of the dark lanes and fields.

The village school was run by a Mr and Mrs Tipper. It had only three classes, Infants, Juniors and Seniors and these were very crowded.

The high point of the village year was haymaking. We all helped. The boys used to rub hay in the girls' faces and kiss them. This was, so they said, in order to make the hay sweet. I am not sure whether this was an authentic country custom, or a joke to fool people of the town.

We knew little about the war, as life in Devon was so peaceful. However I can remember one time when this tranquillity was broken by a plane that crashed in a field nearby.

I spent four happy years at Lane End Farm and I still write to Henry and Mrs Tucker.

Farming became a key factor in the nation's ability to survive, as German U-boats sank more and more of our supply ships crossing the Atlantic. War Agricultural Committees were set up, which instructed farmers as to which crops they should grow and in what quantities. The parish representative was Frank Yendell (senior) who was obliged to report to South Molton Area Committee. Girls from the Women's Land Army were drafted in to help and in the latter years of the war Italian and German prisoners of war also lent a hand.

Top: *A famous wartime cartoon by Low of Ernest Bevin with Winston Churchill, Clement Atlee and other members of the wartime cabinet.*
Above: *In 1981 Rosemary Dobson returned to Lane End Farm and introduced her daughter, Deborah, to Dora and Henry Tucker.*

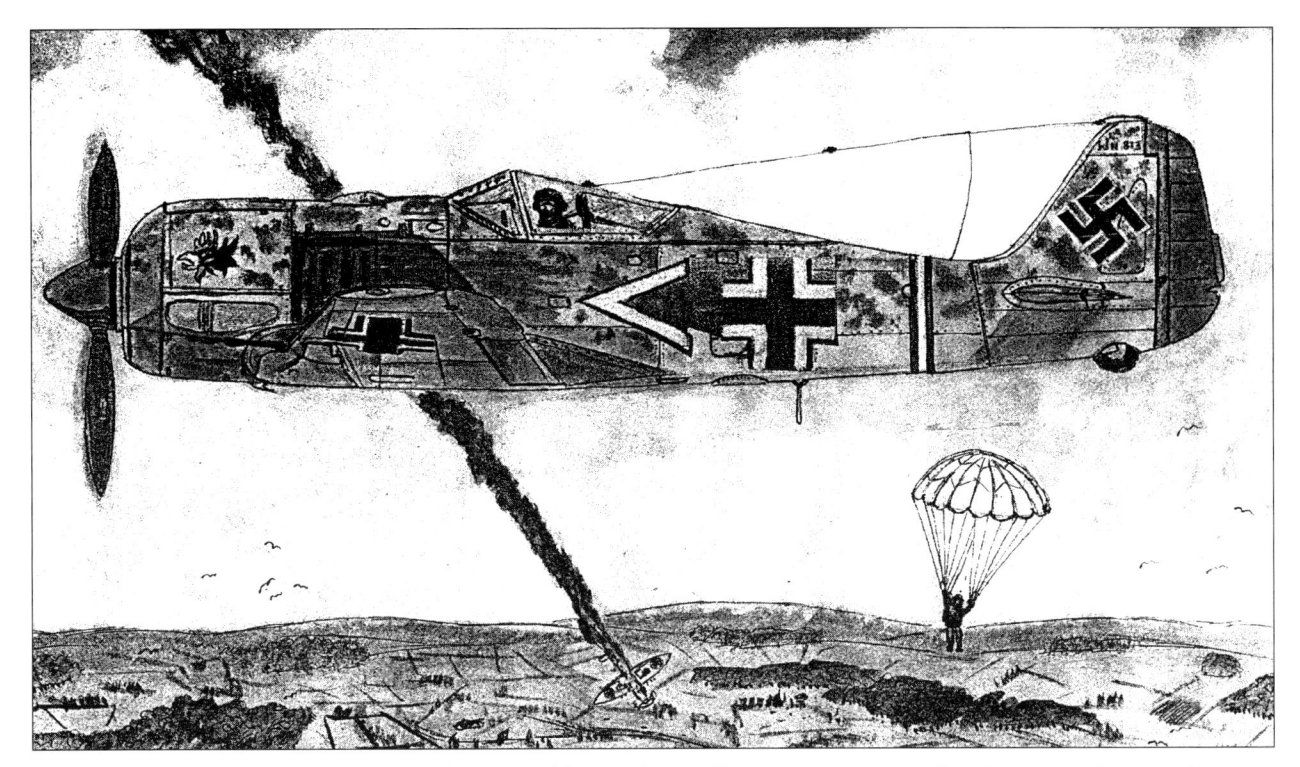

Czech pilot Franzik Trejtnar baling out of his Focke Wulf 190 over West Emlett Farm, 23 June 1942. Drawing by Graham Lewis of Crediton.

The work of the voluntary organisations was considerable, The Women's Institute and the WVS in particular helped by sending Christmas and knitted gifts to the troops overseas, by helping evacuees and running National Savings groups. The WVS ran a meat pie supply service in the village, making a farthing's profit on each pie. After the war the profits were used to buy the six or eight metal seats which are still used in the parish to this day.

In response to the threat of invasion, the government created a Home Guard unit in every village and town throughout the nation. The Morchard Bishop Home Guard numbered in excess of 60 men, all of whom trained at weekends and in the evenings after their normal day's work. Initially equipped with armbands, shotguns and First World War rifles, they were later supplied with uniforms and modern weapons. Numerous stories which circulated suggest that it is surprising none of their members were seriously injured or killed in training, particularly on the grenade and rifle ranges.

Soon after the outbreak of war both Barton House and the Memorial Hall were taken over by the Royal Army Medical Corp and a searchlight unit occupied fields near 'Stone Ash'. The United States 9th Infantry Division was stationed in Tiverton and their troops were a familiar site in the area, mixing regularly with the locals and attending dances at the Memorial Hall. In 1944 this unit was one of the first to land in Normandy and suffered heavy casualties.

Parishioners witnessed a 'dog fight' on the morning of 23 June 1942 between a Spitfire of 310 Squadron based at RAF Exeter (now Exeter airport) and a German Focke Wulf 190 (*above*). The Spitfire was shot down but it's Czechoslovakian pilot, Flight Sergeant Franzik Trejtnar, baled out over West Emlett Farm. One local eyewitness was Norman Snell who tells how, as a lad, he saw this pilot parachuting down and informed an RAF officer who was instructing recruits in the Memorial Hall. Norman and his friends made their way across the fields to Crookstock Farm where they found the Czech pilot hanging in a tree by his parachute. He had broken his arm and was shouting in a foreign language. The boys thought he was German and ran away. Unfortunately, Norman was wearing oversized Wellington boots and he lost one in the mud as he took flight – he never found that boot again.

The German pilot Lt. Armin Farber must have lost his bearings for when he flew over the Bristol Channel he thought he was crossing the English Channel. He was most surprised when

Celebration of Peace

Proposed by Mr Maunder and seconded by Mr Conibeer, that the following expenses incurred in connection with the Celebration of Peace, be defrayed by the Parish Council out of the Poor Rate.

Balance Sheet

Expenditure	£	s	d	Receipts	£	s	d
Fireworks	5	5	-	Advance Mr L Maunder	15	-	-
Drew & Burrow Sports	5	5	-	— Mr Oatway	15	-	-
St Annes Well Brewery				Mr Hayden	15	-	-
9 gallons of Ale	1	-	-	Mr J. Conibeer	12	13	11
Prizes 1st Howard Archway		10	-				
2nd S.L. Southern		7	6	By Sale of Cake & Tea			
Heard Carriage of Ale		2	6	Mrs Buckingham 5¼ lbs at 1/-		5	3
J. Conibeer – Coal and Wood		5	-	Mrs Hill 2¼ lbs at 1/-		2	3
W. Lee Carrying the Flag		2	6	Mrs Hayden 5lbs at 1/-		5	-
C. Drew Bandmaster		3	10	Mrs Cousins 2 1/2lbs & 8 ozs Tea		3	10
E. Way Bread and cakes	5	6	11	Mrs Smith 2lbs cake		3	-
F. Way Do	5	-	7	Mrs Yendell 5lbs cake		5	-
Mrs Philips Tea & Salt		6	-	Mrs Roberts 2lbs cacke & 10oz tea		3	8
Mr Ford Minerals, Tea etc.	1	8	4	Mrs Steer Sale of tea		18	1
Mr Buckingham Milk		1	8				
Mrs Mortimer butter		9	8				
Mr Chanter Ringers	1	10	-				
Mr Burrow Tea		5	-				
Mr Pugsley Do		5	4				
Mr Frost Do		5	4				
Mrs Bennett Do		4	8				
Mr Pike Ale	4	3	-				
Mr Venner Beef	22	7	-				
Mrs Haydon Butter		9	8				
Mr Hill Milk and Butter		6	6				
Mrs Oatway Milk		1	8				
Mrs Yendell Do		1	8				
Mrs Smith Do		1	8				
Mrs Bennett Do		1	8				
Mr Conibeer Stoking the Furnace		6	6				
Mrs Southern Oil		1	-				
Mr Venner Butter		12	6				
Mr Tipper Postage		1	1				
Total	£60	0	0		£60	0	0

he landed at RAF Pembrey in South Wales, to find he was not in Northern France. He spent the next few years as a prisoner of war. The two pilots have met one another on several occasions since the war.

The RAF were delighted with this gift from the Luftwaffe, particularly as they had been planning a commando raid to capture one in Northern France. The plane was immediately stripped down and taken to Farnborough where the authorities learned a lot about this very successful aircraft. This Focke Wulf 190 was to become possibly the most famous of the 190s and part of the fuselage and cockpit is now preserved at an aircraft museum in Shoreham, Kent.

On 30 May the following year a De Haviland Mosquito bomber of 456 squadron from RAF Ford in Hampshire, made a forced landing at Chillingford Farm, Morchard Bishop.

This plane which was built of ply and balsa wood, virtually disintegrated when it hit the ground and both the crew, Wing Commander Dwyer and Pilot Officer Shanks were injured and later taken to hospital in Exeter. Their incredible survival, however, was not the only lucky event of the day; a Morchard girl, Isabelle Woods from nearby Shores, was one several local residents who attended the two wounded men at the scene and she subsequently married Pilot Officer Shanks who took her back to his home in New Zealand, where they kept a sheep farm.

The third aircraft incident occurred at 9.30pm on 15 November the following year, when two Halifax bombers – one from RCAF Wombleton and the other from RCAF Dishforth – collided over Morchard on a training flight. One plane crashed near Crookstock Farm having caught fire. The other landed between Oldborough and Watcombe Farm but the wreckage was not discovered until the following day. From the two crews only one man survived.

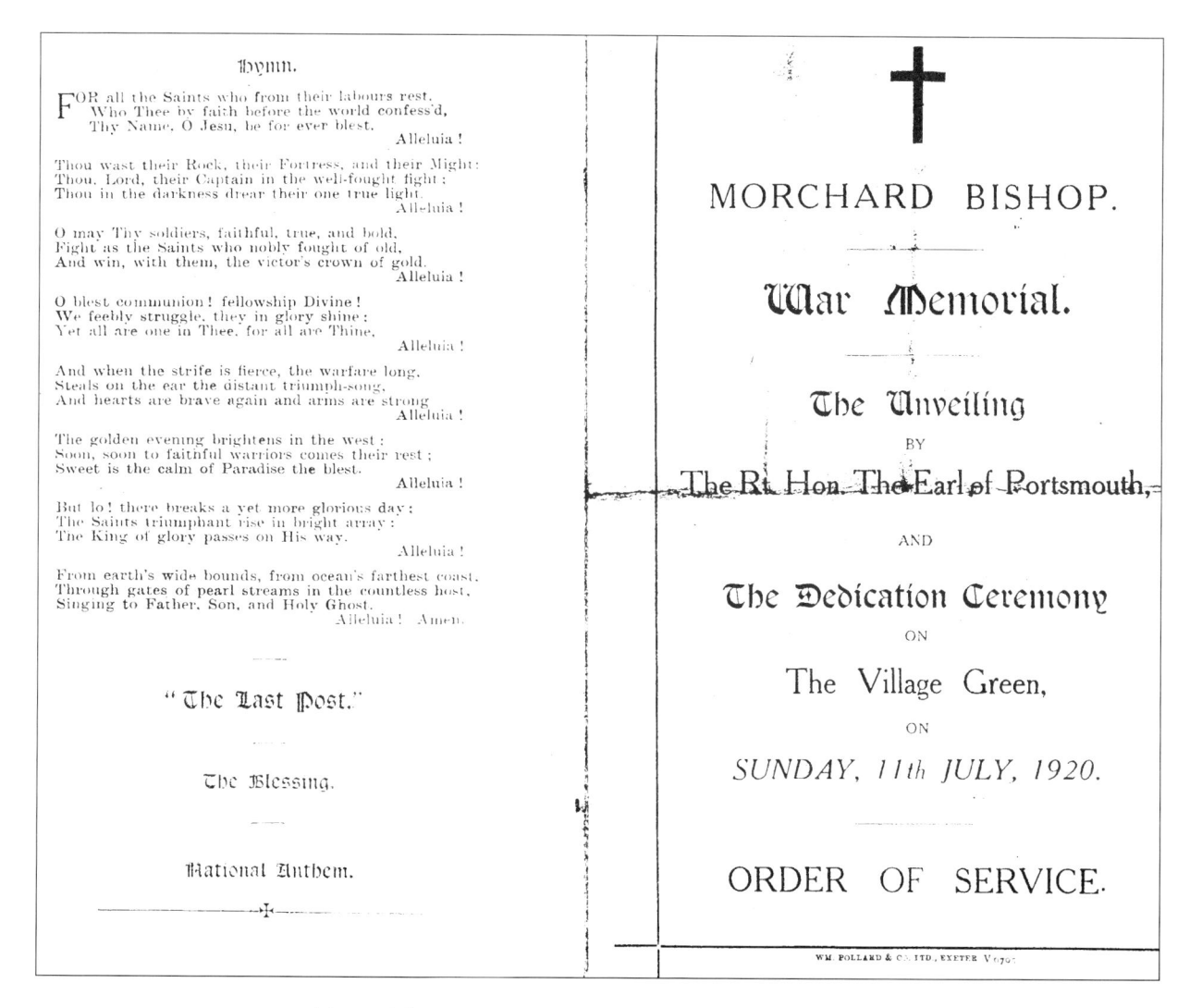

Above: The War Memorial was dedicated on 11 July 1920.

Forever Remembered

Memorial plan for aircrews

THIRTEEN men who died when two RAF bombers collided over Devon in world war two are to have a memorial erected in their honour.

It will be placed on the village green at Morchard Bishop where it will be unveiled and dedicated on Sunday, November 6. The ceremony will mark the 50th anniversary of the horrendous crash over the area on November 15, 1944.

A sister of one of the men who now lives in Canada will be travelling over for the event.

Responsible for the memorial project is Crediton businessman Graham Lewis and fellow members of the South West Aviation Historical Society, who have been busy fundraising to help meet the cost.

Graham said: "We became fascinated by local stories of this dreadful wartime crash and gradually pieced together the history. Thanks to the help of local people we retrieved some remains of the crashed aircraft, including a propeller blade and the flight engineer's instrument panel.

"On that night 50 years ago three Halifax bombers were on a training flight from bases in Yorkshire and were due to turn around over Devon and return. But two of them collided. It was a very cold but clear night and it seems that cockpit screens had iced up, reducing visibility.

"Both crashed in the Morchard area. The third landed at St Eval.

"One of the crashed planes, piloted by Flt Lt Robert Garvie, was crewed by Canadians. The other, flown by Pilot Officer Harrold Pugh, an Ausralian, was crewed by Britons and Australians. Pugh baled out and was he only survivor. He completed his raining but sadly was posted missing just before the end of the war after a raid at Heligoland."

Graham said the crews were all training on heavy four engined aircraft before being posted to active service units.

He had discovered that one crew member, Flt Sgt T. Douris, missed the fatal flight.

"We believe he survived the war and if he is still around we'd love to hear from him," he added.

The memorial has been made for the aviation society by Crediton mason John Stevens and his son Simon.

It will be dedicated by the Rector of Morchard Bishop, the Rev Brian Shillingford, with the minister of the Methodist Church, the Rev Jeff Moles. Among the guests will be Miss Leona Boss, now 90, from Canada, whose brother, Flying Officer Norman Boss, was one of the men who died.

Also taking part will be a representative of the Canadian air defence staff, members of the Aircrew Association, the Royal British Legion and the Exeter St Thomas High School ATC Squadron.

● Donations towards the cost of the memorial can be made at the Lewis Hotpoint Centre, Crediton, Morchard Bishop Post Office or the London Inn, Morchard Bishop.

Pictures by JOHN FOULKES

Extract from the Express and Echo.

Ceremony on 6 November 1994 to mark the 50th anniversary of the crash of the two RAF bombers over Devon. (Left to right) front row: George Bowden, Mervyn Rice, Bill Brown, Norman Snell.

Morchard Bishop Home Guard, 1945.

(Left to right) back row: Cyril Pickard, Theo Watts, Bill Brewer, Albert Veal, Bill Ridd, Will Watts, Sid Rice, Bill Drew, Will Edwards, Will Drew, Ned Hooper, Bill Tancock, Stafford Palfrey, Mr Hosegood;

middle row: Mr Bennett, Fred Down, Gordon Pickard, Aubrey Edwards, Alec Ridd, Henry Tucker, Headly Glover, Jack Pugsley, Stanley Drew, Cecil Ridd, Charlie Smith, Mr Petherick, Bernard Saunders, Jack Barnet, Alfie Rice, John Mears, Wilfred Rice, Archie Tucker, George Burrou, Bill Mildon, John Cann, Bob Cann, Archie Partridge, Headley Chapple, Harold Webber;

front row: Wilfred Elworthy, Bill Elworthy, Tom Cann, Reg Ford, Mr Symes, Col. Rodwell, Erne Edworthy, Bert Brimilcombe, Aston Otton, Joe Hole, Frank Land.

Commonwealth War Grave Commission
In Memory of Charles Albert Bennett Private 5618136
1st Bn., Devonshire Regiment who died on Tuesday, 11th April 1944.
Commemorative Information

Memorial: RANGOON MEMORIAL, Myanmar/Grave Reference/ Face 6/Panel Number:
Location: The Rangoon Memorial is situated in Taukkyan War Cemetery, which is outside Yangon (formerly Rangoon), near the airport and immediately adjoining the village of Taukkyan. It is on the Prome Road, about 35 kilometres north of the city, from which it is easily accessible. The Memorial stands in the centre of the Cemetery, surrounded by the graves of more than 6000 men who fought and died with those whom it commemorates, whose remains were brought from the battlefield cemeteries at Akyab, Mandalay, Meiktila and Sahmaw, and from scattered jungle and roadside graves all over Burma. It is in the form of two long open garden courts flanked by covered walks and joined by an open rotunda. The names of the fallen are carved on the inner faces of broad rectangular piers placed at intervals to form the sides of the covered walks. Through these colonnades can be seen the green lawns of the cemetery and the colourful garden courts. On the frieze inside the rotunda are inscribed in English these words:
1939-1945 HERE ARE RECORDED THE NAMES OF TWENTY SEVEN
THOUSAND SOLDIERS OF MANY RACES UNITED IN SERVICE TO THE
BRITISH CROWN WHO GAVE THEIR LIVES IN BURMA AND ASSAM BUT TO
WHOM THE FORTUNE OF WAR DENIED THE CUSTOMARY RITES
ACCORDED TO THEIR COMRADES IN DEATH

Also engraved on the rotunda in English, Bunnese, Hindi, Urdu and Gurinuidil is the inscription:
THEY DIED FOR ALL FREE MEN

British Legion Dinner, c.1938.
The group includes: F. Chudley, F. Stentiford, F. Northam, P. Andrews, T. Oatway Snr, J. Warren, Reg Ford, Sid Rice, W. Holland, Mr Bowie, Mrs Chudley.

T. Oatway makes a presentation to Joe Burrow before his departure from the village in 1957.

Chapter 12: Sport and Recreation

Over the passing of the years Morchard Bishop has maintained a strongly-held place in the forefront of sport, and today it boasts some of the finest facilities (most of them having been developed since the end of Second World War) of any village in the county.

Rugby was played on the field called 'Ackmoran' opposite Greenways up until 1907 and tennis and bowling took place between the wars in the Old Rectory. Football and horse racing, meanwhile, were enjoyed at The Parks behind Polson Hill Garage, up until 1939. This was also the site of the annual village fair but for some reason this facility was not available after 1940, and the village also lacked a playing field. At the turn of the century and up till 1939 cricket was played on the field behind the school.

In December 1949 Joe Burrow and other members of the Ex-servicemen's Association complained to the Parish Council that there was no public playing field in the village. Thanks to the efforts of the Rev. Rushbridger and Brigadier Barker-Benfield, a lease was drawn up two months later between Heathcote Estate, Mr Yendell and the Parish Council, to use the field behind the school as a playing field.

Enthusiasts bought and erected an old wartime Nissen hut as a changing room, laid on water and rolled the area using a steam roller. It was described as one of the best playing fields in the area.

The opening of the playing field in the old Cricket Field at Wood Barton, May 1950.
Left to right: M. Huchings, D. Tipper, F. Yendell, T. Oatway, George Lambert, Mrs Lambert, Brigadier Barker-Benfield.

Sports Facilities

In 1957 thanks to various donations, the Morchard Bishop Playing Field Association was set up and the present five-acre site in Wood Lane was purchased, the site fenced and levelled and a small pavilion built.

In 1978, Miss Hazelton (Brigadier Barker-Benfield's housekeeper) left a legacy of £19,000 for the playing field and shortly after Mrs D. M. Oliver, a former treasurer of the association, bequeathed £3400 in her will.

The next few years saw lots of improvements – a new tennis court (*opposite centre*) was built, the children's play area developed (*right*), the pavilion extended (*bottom*), a bar added and the welcome addition of new changing facilities made.

Thanks to the efforts of Geoff Rice, Gill Gunn, Mike Jeffries and the late Shirley Brewer and other volunteers, a very successful sports set-up developed and at one stage there were two football teams, a cricket team, a ladies netball team, a tennis club and a tug-of-war team. The Sports Club also ran two skittles teams, darts and pool teams.

The opening of the playing field at Wood Barton, 1950.

Top to bottom: the childrens' play area, hard court, and pavilion.

Morchard Fayre

The Morchard Fayre is still held annually, even if in a rather less helter-skelter manner than in pre-war days when it was held in the field opposite Polson Hill garage. Since the late 1950s it has been sited in the new playing field, with the assistance of most of the village organisations who take on responsibility for a stall or function. Since 1996 it has included a rally involving vintage vehicles and pieces of equipment.

Left: The organisers. Left to right: Geoff Rice, Ron Bendall, Phil Bourne, Terry Nott, Bobby Robinson.

Below: 1996 – ITV West Country Weatherman Ron Bendall with the fancy dress parade.

Village Cricket

Joe Burrow with the Cricket Team in 1952.

Morchard Bishop Cricket Team 1989. (Left to right) back row: Alan Carbert, Tim Schofield, Julian Rice, Keith Bolt, Eric Taylor, Steve Rice, Jeff Hooper, Nick Heath; front: George Burrow, Maurice Le May, Roy Amor, Roger Quick, Wyn Staite, Graham Keen, Ken Vere.

Morchard Footballers

The football club was reformed after the war, but they did not have the necessary kit and the clothing rationing which was still in force prevented them from buying anything new. This problem was solved thanks to the efforts and admirable ingenuity of Mrs Muriel Heale (née Scott) and other ladies who collected the, by then unwanted, black-out curtains from villagers for the team kit. The ladies made the shirts and George and Joe Burrow made the shorts, and the Morchard Bishop All Blacks took to the field.

The Football Team 1982/3
(Left to right) back row: Geoff Rice, Darren Sandercock, Martyn Dockings, Jonathan Bradford, Peter Mead, Kevin Rice, Richard Parkhouse, Julian Rice, Steve Baker;
Front row: Mark Bradford, Micky Phelan, Andrew Rice, Andrew Haydon, Charles Parkhouse, Mark Rice.

2nd XI 1994/5.
(Left to right) back row: Martyn Dockings, Jonathan Bradford, Andrew Rice, Michael Bourne, Darren Sandercock, Rob Brealy;
front row: Michael Tapp, Martin Daniel, Michael Close, Christopher Peters, Peter Bradfield, Andrew Hayden.

First XI 1994/5.
(Left to right) back row: Rob Brealy (Manager), Mark Bradford, Jonathan Bradford, Daniel Mason, Terry Taylor, Steven Rice, Michael Tapp, Trevor Vickery (linesman), Ray Burrow;
front row: Kevin Rice, Mark Rice, Paul Gribble, George Burrow (President), Scott Brimilcombe, Martin Brealy, Graham Hooper.

The Bowling Club

The Mid Devon Council was obviously very impressed with what the village had achieved and offered to build a bowling green on the site if the village paid £1000 towards the cost. The green was built at a cost in the region of £40,000 and was officially opened on 29 April 1984 by the District Council Chairman.

Unfortunately the winter and spring of 1984 was one of the driest on record and the expensive Cumberland turf which had not bedded in, soon deteriorated. Once again the village's inadequate water pressure was to become a problem, so water had to be brought in by milk tanker from Oldborough and Bugford quarries on at least six occasions, to save the precious turf.

Temporary changing accommodation was provided by way of an old Portakabin until the newly-formed Bowling Club could find enough money and muscle to build their own facilities.

Left: One vital question – "How do you drive a digger across a bowling green without damaging the precious turf?"

Below: Everything stops for tea! Jeff Kingaby and Sue O'Brien

Bottom: Eric Brewer taking a break.

Opposite page Clockwise from far left: Voluntary labour was the order of the day – Edwin Hutchings; work proceeds on the new dressing rooms; water, electricity and sewerage from the main club house were connected to the Portakabin and new toilet block

The Bowling Club

The opening ceremony. Left to right: Molly Kingaby (Ladies' Secretary), Cllr David Pugsley (Chairman Mid Devon District Council), Tony Bond (President Devon County Bowling Association), Cllr Roger Quick (Mid Devon District Council), Sybil Williams, Nicola Poole (Ladies' Captain), Mike Jeffery (Chairman MB Bowling Club), Rev. Brian Shillingford.

Time to relax!

Chapter 12: A Morchard Miscellany

The township of Morchard in Southern Australia was proclaimed in August 1877. It was named by Sir Samuel Way, after the village of Morchard Bishop in North Devon where his father, the Rev. James Way was born and brought up, and where his forefathers had lived for hundreds of years. The last member of the Way family died in Morchard Bishop in 1966.

Sir Samuel Way, Q.C. who was the Chief Justice and First Lieutenant Governor of South Australia at the time, and had been Chancellor of the University of Adelaide, was credited with introducing Shropshire sheep into Australia.

Our thanks to The Morchard District (Australia) Centenary Book Committee 1976 (ISBN 0 9597326 0 8) who provided information and the photographs shown on page 142 and also Joan Ellery of the Country Womens Association (The Australian W.I.) who are in regular contact with our own W.I. members.

A view of Church Street in Morchard Bishop, Devon, during the 1930s showing the vegetable gardens to the right.

Morchard Store, Southern Australia.

Morchard, Southern Australia.

The Sale of the Century

Not many villages can claim that the vast majority of their village was sold by auction on one day. Prior to 9 April 1909 almost all the village was glebe land and owned by the Bishop, with the exception of all the properties from the Congregational Chapel down as far as, and including, the terraced houses in Chulmleigh Road. Although these premises were all privately owned, many of the front gardens opposite the green were glebe property. (Interestingly, both the Congregational Chapel and the Methodist Chapel were not built on the glebe.).

On that one-day Tatepath Farm, 'The London Hotel' as it was then called, and 49 houses and cottages and numerous pieces of land through the village were sold. The auction didn't start till 1.30pm and one wonders what time they could have finished. Although the sale prices are not recorded, the annual rents are interesting.

Lot 41, which is now Woodstock, Julian Rice's joiner's shop next door, and land on which Ben Rhydding and Barnaloft stand, were then described as 'A Superior Dwelling House, A Two Roomed Cottage and one rod and twenty poles of land'. The annual rent was £17.10s. (£17.50) per annum.

Lot 5 was described as 'An Excellent Arable Field called Little Merchants (at Merchants Corner) containing 1 acre, 3 rods and 8 perches at an annual rent of £2 per annum'. This sold for £55.

MORCHARD BISHOP, DEVON.

Particulars, with Plans and Conditions of Sale

OF

FREEHOLD

Lands, Houses and Cottages,

Situate in and adjoining the Village of Morchard Bishop, about 2 miles from Morchard Road Station, on the North Devon Line of the London and South Western Railway Company, and Seven miles from the Town of Crediton,

being portions of the Rectorial Glebe of the Parish of Morchard Bishop, and comprising

A Compact and Productive Farm,

KNOWN AS

"TATEPATH,"

A fully-licensed Inn,

CALLED

"THE LONDON HOTEL"

Valuable Accommodation, Pasture, and Arable Fields,

AND

49 HOUSES AND COTTAGES,

THE WHOLE CONTAINING

162 a. 0r. 20 p.,

To be offered for SALE BY AUCTION.

At the LONDON HOTEL, MORCHARD BISHOP

BY

Mr. C.J. HANNAFORD,

On THURSDAY, the 9th day of April, 1908
at 1.30 o'clock precisely

Particulars, with Plans and Conditions of Sale, maybe obtained of the AUCTIONEER, Chulmleigh, North Devon;
Messrs Sparkes, Pope & Thomas, Solicitors, Crediton & Exeter;
Messrs. T.C. & G.F. Kellock, Solicitors, Totnes;
or of Messrs J. & R. Drew, Land Agents, Surveyors, 15 Queens St., Exeter.

Public notice for the auction on 9 April 1909.

The Morchard Club Procession at the turn of the century.

Baker Way (whose bakery was in Fore Street) with his bread cart in 1914 and 14-year-old Charles Rice (holding the horse). Charles later married Nellie Dicker and lived with her at the Old Rectory Lodge where they raised 12 children.

Freda Heggadon (left) and Mary Rice (right, now Cornish) selling flowers at the Church Fête, Beech Hill 1936/7.

Morchard from the air.

The Old Post Office, Church Street, 1906.

The Skimmity Ride

In 1914 Jack Tolley ran the village Post Office but when a married woman named Mabel moved in with him, the village people objected. Tom and Alf Bennett went down to the slaughter house and filled an ox bladder with blood which he shot all over the front walls of the Post Office. Others put tar and feathers on the building. Then they called out the village band and paraded effigies of Jack and Mabel around the village. Finally they went behind the Congregational Chapel and burnt the effigies. The couple ran off to Exeter to live.

The author Thomas Hardy describes a similar incident to this in his book *The Mayor of Casterbridge* in which he describes a 'skimmity ride'. This was apparently a common west-country way of showing public disapproval and, although there was a similar event in North Devon in the 1930s, the Morchard incident is possibly one of the last known in the county.

Sketch by Julie Rudge

Fire!

A total of 13 people were made homeless just before Christmas 1938 when four cottages at Redhills, Morchard Bishop, were totally destroyed. The well water at the cottages was insufficient to have any impact on the flames and the only other alternative water source was over a mile away.

The flames, which were fanned by an icy north-easterly gale at 8.45 on the morning of 18 December, soon swept across the expanse of thatch and when the Crediton fire brigade arrived within an hour at 9.30 most of the furniture inside the cottages had also been destroyed.

A Fire at Wigham Farm in 1984, when the building was extensively damaged. Due to snow the fire brigade had difficulty reaching the fire.

The house has now been fully restored and provides an excellent example of a traditional thatch and cob building.
The owners Dawn and Stephen Chilcott won the 1998 Best Bed and Breakfast award for the South West of England

Before and after the fire at Morchard Green, 22 August 1907.

VE Day, 8 May 1995

In March 1945 the Ministry of Local Government sent out a circular to all local authorities stating that as the war in Europe was coming to an end, they should make plans to celebrate. Most towns and villages had large parties. But in the case of Morchard Bishop, it is recorded (in the Parish Council minutes) that the response to this request was 'we won't worry about that just now'. It took the village 50 years to arrange their celebration but when the day finally arrived it was certainly well worth waiting for.

This page: The day began with a fancy dress parade and included a salute to the village from an RAF Hercules.

Main picture, opposite: Even the weather behaved itself for the children's tea party in Church Street.

Morchard Bishop
Souvenir Programme
and Village Directory

Celebrating the 50th Anniversary of "VE" Day 1945

Price £1.50 p.

Left: A Souvenir Programme and Village Directory with 50 pages was produced, of which some 750 copies were sold.

Mrs Wheeley, who contributed so much to the Memorial Hall both in funds and effort over the years, is presented with a bouquet (by Anne Jones) after unveiling a plaque to commemorate VE Day.

VE Day, 8 May 1995

Top: Members of the British Legion, including Ray Burrow (far left), Bert Bowden (4th from left) and Reg Land (5th from left).

Above: A sing-song in the Memorial Hall.

Left: We light a beacon to celebrate the end of a perfect day.

A Wedding role for Devon Yeoman

On 29 July 1981, the nation prepared to celebrate as the wedding day of Prince Charles and Lady Diana Spencer finally arrived.

Among those attending the event were thousands upon thousands of well-wishers, many of them from the ranks of the rich and famous, many more from the general public.

Only a lucky few were assured a close-up view of the proceedings and among them was a Morchard man with a strange and ancient 'title'. Numbering among the Queen's closest bodyguards, Robert (Bob) Layfield of Seethington Cottage, Morchard Bishop, was one of around 30 members of the Queen's Bodyguard of the Yeoman of the Guard who attended the royal wedding at St Pauls Cathedral.

The wedding was one of the most important events Mr Layfield had been called upon to attend in his 24 years of duty in the corps and only two years earlier, in 1979, he was awarded the prestigious Insignia of the Royal Victorian Order.

Other state duties of the Bodyguard include attendance at banquets, receptions, garden parties and investitures as well as the opening of Parliament.

The oldest surviving military corps in the world, the Bodyguard was founded by Henry VII in 1485 and today members still wear Tudor uniforms similar to those of the Beefeaters. They are split into two main ranks – 'yeoman bedgoers' of which Mr Layfield was one, and 'yeoman bed-hangers'. The bed-goers were required to taste all the food before the monarch and to jump up and down on the royal bed to ensure that there were no daggers hidden amongst the covers. The bed-hangers meanwhile made a thorough search of the drapery to make sure that nobody was lurking there ready to pounce!

Murder at Morchard Bishop

Trelawny is one of the oldest cottages in the village – it also has one of the most disturbing histories! When David Page was told that a murder had taken place in his newly-aquired retreat, these were the facts he uncovered:

George Godbeare Tapp was the second of seven children born to William and Thomazin Godbeare. Thomazin was illiterate and put her mark on the parish register instead of signing it. William died in 1802 and George, the eldest son, took over his father's responsibility for his mother, three sisters and three brothers.

George was a labourer. Those of his family who could work were handed loom weavers. Times were hard. The whole family was crowded into what was then a 'one up, one down', thatched cottage where the weavers probably worked. At some time George began using the alias Tapp, although the reason remains unclear as presumably his true name Godbeare was known in the village (George Tapp bears is no relation of the Tapp family currently living in the village).

In 1808 George was 28, and his friend Robert Leach, a butcher, was 23. George owed him money. Robert was last seen alive drinking with George in a public house near the cottage on the evening of Sunday 24 April 1808. They were seen to leave together and Leach then disappeared.

His family became very concerned about his disappearance because he had been carrying some £60 in cash at the time. Suspicion fell on George Tapp, who subsequently appeared to have been spending more money than usual. It also transpired that he had been seen, late on the previous Saturday evening, digging a deep pit in his garden – at the time he had explained that it was for dung for his cucumbers! The pit was dug up on the following Saturday and found to contain the body of Robert Leach. He had an axe wound to the back of his head three inches long and two inches deep. George was arrested and confessed to the crime. He had planned the murder a week before and the motive was robbery.

What George's mother's involvement in the crime was remains unclear but she appeared with her son at the Exeter Assizes held at Exeter Castle in August of that year. It is difficult to imagine how George carried out the murder without anyone else in the house knowing about it but Thomazin was discharged 'for want of prosecution'. George, meanwhile, was hanged in public at Exeter on Tuesday 16 August 1808.

The Orange People

This controversial group, named after their distinctive orange clothing, are members of the Sannysain movement consisting of more than 250,00 disciples of the Indian mystic, Bhagwan Shree Rajneesh. In 1981 they celebrated the coming of autumn with a three-day, non-stop music festival at Beech Hill which they renamed 'The mansion of Prempanthan – Path of Love'.

When the Morchard centre closed down, some the followers moved on to the 65,000 acre 'Big Muddy Ranch' near Antelope, Oregon, which became internationally known for its problems.

'Guess the Weight of Brigadier Barker-Benfield' at the church fête, Beech Hill, late 1950s. Rev. Rushbridger appears behind the weighing machine and Thomas Galway is on the right.

Crowds gather for a visit to Morchard by the M.P. George Lambert, 1908.

Subscribers

Mrs Greta Abbott (née Tucker), Cowplain, Hampshire
Ann Adams, Zeal Monachorum, Crediton, Devon
Royston & Jane Amor, Malvern, Worcs.
Mr Bill Andrews, Chawleigh, Crediton, Devon
Mrs Jean Andrews, Morchard Bishop, Devon
Sonja & Colin Andrews, Morchard Bishop, Devon
Greg & Frances Anson, Frost, Morchard Bishop, Devon
Julian Bahlmann & Angela Smith, Brisbane, Australia
Christine Bailey, Morchard Bishop, Devon
Vic & Patricia Balsdon, Morchard Bishop, Devon
John, Carri, Daryl & Carly Bartle, Morchard Bishop, Devon
Beech Hill Community Co-Operative, Morchard Bishop, Devon
Margaret Bell, Wellingborough, Northamptonshire
Brian & Lorraine Bewsher, Buckfastleigh, Devon
Phil & Mary Bourne & Family, Morchard Bishop, Devon
Jean Claude & Francoise Boutigny, St Gatien Des Bois, Normandy, France
Barbara M. Bowden, Morchard Bishop, Devon
Mr R. Bradford, Morchard Bishop, Devon
Mr G. J. Bragg, Tiverton, Devon
Rachel Brah, Feltham, Middlesex
Mervyn K. Brewer, Perth, Western Australia
Pamela D. Brimilcombe, Morchard Bishop, Devon
Bert Brimilcombe, Morchard Bishop, Devon
Robert J. Brooks, Morchard Bishop, Devon
W. H. C. Brown, Morchard Bishop, Devon
Peter Brownson, Sydney
Raymond Brownson, Durham
Brigadier Derek Brownson CBE, Abingdon, Oxon
Peter & Linda Buck, Morchard Bishop, Devon
Gwen Buckingham, Morchard Bishop, Devon
Mrs Sheila Burak, Morchard Bishop, Devon
David Burks, Eggesford Gardens, Chulmleigh, Devon
Captain L. E. Burrell M.B.E., Morchard Bishop, Devon
Ian Burrow, Crowthorne, Berkshire
K. J. Burrow, Bucks Cross, Bideford, Devon
J. W. & D. L. Burrow, Paignton, Devon
Ray Burrow, Morchard Bishop, Devon
Gerald J. Burrow, Morchard Bishop, Devon
Mr Colin C. Burrow, Black Dog, Crediton, Devon
Janice & Terry Butler, Morchard Bishop, Devon
Mrs Joan Bywater,
Mr P. J. Cann, Oxfordshire
Peter Cann, Morchard Bishop, Devon
Ann Cann, Crediton, Devon
Margaret Baker & Terry Cann, Morchard Bishop, Devon
Christopher A. J. Cann, Coleford, Crediton, Devon
David & Dawn Cann, Crediton, Devon
Alan Carbert, Morchard Bishop, Devon
Tom & Maureen Carr, Morchard Bishop, Devon
C. E. G. Carrington, Morchard Bishop, Devon
Paul & Gill Carter
Stephen Carter (Postmaster), Morchard Bishop, Devon
Mrs M. Chapple, Morchard Bishop, Devon
Dawn, Steve & Alistair Chilcott, Morchard Bishop, Devon
Jean Cole (née Phillips), Swindon, Wiltshire
Phil & Ray Colton, Morchard Bishop, Devon
Hazel Connell (née Brewer), Crediton, Devon
Raymond C. Cook, Morchard Bishop, Devon
Mrs Sonia Coombes, Rochester, Kent
Miss Julia D. Cousins, Bournmouth
Mr & Mrs B. J. Cousins, Copplestone, Devon
Margaret Cousins, St Saviours, Crediton, Devon
O. B. Cox, East Worlington, Crediton, Devon
Peter C. B. Craske, California, USA
Mr M. C. & Mrs J. C. Curgenven, Morchard Bishop, Devon
Bob & Maureen Davies, Morchard Bishop, Devon
Rosemary Dobson (née Hobbs), Surrey
Gordon W. Dockings, Southcott Farm, Morchard Bishop, Devon
Martyn J. Dockings, Southbourne, Morchard Bishop, Devon
Mr & Mrs Henry Dockings, Morchard Bishop, Devon
Edward & Jenny Down, Queensland, Australia
George & Marina Down, Watcombe Farm, Morchard Bishop, Devon
Mrs P. Down, Copplestone, Crediton, Devon
Mrs P. D. Edwards, Copplestone, Crediton, Devon
Aubrey Edwards, Morchard Bishop, Devon
Douglas & Pamela Ellis, Lydcott, Morchard Bishop, Devon
Neville P. Enderson, Coleford, Crediton, Devon
Tony Evans, Tiverton, Devon
J. A. Ewins, Morchard Bishop, Devon
Diana Farrant, Morchard Bishop, Devon
Stephen Fawcett, Taunton, Somerset
Jean Ann Findlay, Morchard Bishop, Devon
The Hon. E. & Mrs E. FitzRoy, Morchard Bishop, Devon
B. L. & S. A. Flynn, Morchard Bishop, Devon
Vivien Forster, Down St Mary,

Crediton, Devon
Vicki Fowler, Chesham, Bucks
Audrey J. Frampton, Morchard Bishop, Devon
Richard Frost, Morchard Bishop, Devon
Eric H. Frost, Morchard Bishop, Devon
Susan Gales (former head teacher), Morchard Bishop, Devon
Nigel & Jacquie Galton, Lapford, Crediton, Devon
Ewen Garner, Australia
Martin & Linda Gillbard, Deneridge Farm, Morchard Bishop, Devon
Lucy Anne Glover, Morchard Bishop, Devon
Mrs M. E. Glover, Copplestone, Crediton, Devon
Mr & Mrs Harry Goodland, Morchard Bishop, Devon
Mr A. Grant, Crediton, Devon
David, Gillian & Richard Gunn, Morchard Bishop, Devon
Mrs Sheila Gurl, Morchard Bishop, Devon
Mrs D. M. Hayes, Clayhanger, Tiverton, Devon
Susan Heady, New York
Charles & Muriel Heal, Morchard Bishop, Devon
Sonia A. Heath, Morchard Bishop, Devon
Mrs F. M. Heggadon, Morchard Bishop, Devon
Tony & Liz Hill, Morchard Bishop, Devon
Ken & Jan Hinchliffe, Morchard Bishop, Devon
Roger Holloway, Morchard Bishop, Devon
Mrs J. Horwill, Heavitree, Exeter, Devon
Mrs C. Howard, Morchard Bishop, Devon
Victoria Hughes, Morchard Bishop, Devon
James & Anna Hughes, Morchard Bishop, Devon
Tracey & Mark Hutchings, Kantara, Morchard Bishop, Devon
Chris & Carol Hutchings, Kantara, Morchard Bishop, Devon
Felicity Hutchings, Morchard Bishop, Devon

Carol M. Isaac, Sandford, Devon
Sue Jackson, Exeter, Devon
Louis James, Northwood Cottage, Morchard Bishop, Devon
Brenda S. James, Morchard Bishop, Devon
Mr B. C. Jarvis, Knowle, Crediton, Devon
Mr M. W. Jeffery, Morchard Bishop, Devon
Anne & Howard Jones, Morchard Bishop, Devon
Terry & Susan Jones, Morchard Bishop, Devon
Mr K. Jones, Oxford
Megan & Lloyd Jones, Morchard Bishop, Devon
Jennifer Jury
Graham Keene, Morchard Bishop, Devon
Mr R. G. Knight, Morchard Bishop, Devon
Lisa & Kenneth Kristensen, Norway
Sandra E. Lake (née Taylor), Morchard Bishop, Devon
Jonathan & Sue Laker, Morchard Bishop, Crediton, Devon
Reginald F. Land, Exeter, Devon
Madge & Bob Layfield (ex Wreford), Morchard Bishop, Devon
Mrs A. N. Leach, Yeoford, Crediton, Devon
Fred & Pat Leat, Morchard Bishop, Devon
Richard Lethbridge, Chittlehamholt, Umberleigh, Devon
G. C. Lewis, Morchard Bishop, Devon
Mrs Christian Lidstone (née Burrow), Perthshire, Scotland
Kate Lowe & Kim Heath, Kalamunda
John & Ida Lucas, Morchard Bishop, Devon
Pam & Ian Macey, Squirrel Lodge, Morchard Bishop, Devon
A. H. Manley & Louis James, Spirelake Cottage, Morchard Bishop, Devon
John Martin, Exeter, Devon
Mrs Alexandra Mason,
Gavin Matthews, Exeter, Devon
George Matthews, Morchard Bishop, Devon

Michael Matthews, Exeter, Devon
Trevor Matthews, Wantage, Oxon
Chrissie J. Maynard (née Tucker), Sutton, Surrey
Karan Meechan, Morchard Bishop, Devon
Florence M. Mildon, Morchard Bishop, Devon
Rachel H. Mills, Lapford, Devon
Adrian D. Mills, Lapford, Devon
Stephen Mills, Rudge Farm, Lapford, Devon
David & Marion Mills, Lapford, Crediton, Devon
Marcia J. Mills (née Rice), Lapford, Devon
Mr & Mrs J. Modzelewski, Morchard Bishop, Devon
Rev. Jeff Moles, Tavistock, Devon
John & Katherine Montgomery, Morchard Bishop, Devon
Maurice & Jean Moore, Morchard Bishop, Devon
Morchard Bishop Recycling Group, Morchard Bishop, Devon
Sheila Nadim, Hope Cottage, Morchard Bishop, Devon
Mrs Kathleen Norris, Perivale, Middlesex
Mary North, Morchard Bishop, Devon
Steven & Bridget North, Morchard Bishop, Devon
Mrs Patricia Oliver, Morchard Bishop, Devon
Ken & Alison Orchard, Crediton, Devon
Caroline Parkhouse, Morchard Bishop, Devon
Charles, Dawn & Jack Parkhouse, Morchard Bishop, Devon
Patricia Parkinson, Ouston
J. Parsonage, Morchard Bishop, Devon
Keith F. Partridge, Morchard Bishop, Devon
Hilda M. Partridge, Morchard Bishop, Devon
Mr Michael E. Partridge, Morchard Bishop, Devon
John A. Partridge, Romford, Essex
Chris Partridge, Lewes, Sussex

THE BOOK OF MORCHARD BISHOP

Les & Caroline Partridge, Broadgate Farm, Morchard Bishop, Devon
Mrs D. Passmore, Barris, Crediton, Devon
Bob & Jacqueline Patten, Morchard Bishop, Devon
Mrs Katrina Paul (née Rudge), Morchard Bishop, Devon
Mrs J. Pentith, Blackpool
Mrs J. C. Pettyfer, Morchard Bishop, Devon
Mr & Mrs J. A. Phillips, North Wingfield, Chesterfield
Mrs P. J. Pickard, Morchard Bishop, Devon
Christopher Pinn, Leeds
Lt Col R Pope, Morchard Bishop, Devon
Janice & Russell Powell, Morchard Bishop, Devon
Dr D. F. Presland, Morchard Bishop, Devon
Claire Proietti, Morchard Bishop, Devon
David Pugsley, Cullompton, Devon
Mr & Mrs K. G. Rice, Morchard Bishop, Devon
Mr R. V. G. Rice, Bishops Castle, Shropshire
Mervyn & Joyce Rice, Morchard Bishop, Devon
Mrs M. Rice, Morchard Bishop, Devon
Mr & Mrs G. A. Rice, Morchard Bishop, Devon
Norman & Yvonne Rice, Morchard Bishop, Devon
Mr L. J. Rice, Morchard Bishop, Devon
Mr P. and Mrs L. Rice, Lapford, Crediton, Devon
Mr & Mrs Mark Rice, Crediton, Devon
Kathleen Rice (née Bowie), Morchard Bishop/Witheridge, Devon
Lewis Richards, Crediton, Devon
D. M. Richards, Honiton, Devon
Annie & Ian Robinson, Morchard Bishop, Devon
Bob Robinson, Morchard Bishop, Devon
John & Fiona Robinson, Morchard Bishop, Devon
David R Robinson, Higher Oldborough, Morchard Bishop, Devon
Mrs Sarah E. Robinson, Higher Oldborough, Morchard Bishop, Devon
Janet A. Rowley, Weeke Barton, Morchard Bishop, Devon
Mrs Julie & Mr Lawson Rudge, Morchard Bishop, Devon
Keza Rudge, North Cornwall
Mrs C. Sandercock, Morchard Bishop, Devon
Mr A. Sanders, Bow, Crediton, Devon
Mrs Wyn Saunders, Crediton, Devon
Derek & Jo Savage, Morchard Bishop, Devon
Victoria Jane Scott, Chulmleigh, Devon
Mrs C. Mary Shears (née Tucker), Wells, Somerset
Mr & Mrs A. P. Sheath, Templeton, Tiverton, Devon
Brian & Kay Shillingford, Morchard Bishop, Devon
Mrs E. M. Shipton, Lapford, Crediton, Devon
Jenny & Dudley Smith, Byways, Morchard Bishop, Devon
Elaine & Mike Smith, Broadclyst, Exeter, Devon
Norman & Helen Snell, Morchard Bishop, Devon
John & Eira Snell, Fountain Meadow, Morchard Bishop, Devon
E. D. Snell, Morchard Bishop, Devon
Family of the late Muriel Sparke, Morchard Bishop, Devon
Bernard Spaughton, Cheam, Surrey
Mrs S. Spottiswoode, Morchard Bishop, Devon
Robin & Caroline Stoyle (née Mills), Crediton, Devon
Sylvia & Richard Suckling
Janet Symons, Morchard Bishop, Devon
Mrs J. K. Targett, Salisbury, Wilts.
Paul A. T. Taylor, North Shields
Mrs M. R. Taylor, Morchard Bishop, Devon
Mrs H. G. Tilney, Morchard Bishop, Devon
Martin & Denise Toms, Morchard Bishop, Devon
Stephen, Elizabeth, Mitchell & Joshua Trott, Torquay, Devon
Graham, Melanie, Emily & Alice Trott, London
John & Doreen Trott (née Rice), Newton Abbot, Devon
P. Brian Tucker, Wellington, Somerset
Major R. T. F. Tucker, E. Yorkshire
Henry & Dora Tucker, Lane End Farm, Morchard Bishop, Devon
Mr David Tucker, Denmead, Hampshire
Peter & Helen Turner, Morchard Bishop, Devon
Betty Turner (née Richards), Exeter, Devon
C.S., T., K.V. & K.L. Tyldesley, Morchard Bishop, Devon
Michael & Mary Tyler, Morchard Bishop, Devon
Kelvin & Julie Varney, Morchard Bishop, Devon
Deirdre Vere, Moor Farm, Morchard Bishop, Devon
George S. Ward, Morchard Bishop, Devon
Ruth Warren, Exeter, Devon
Brian C. Warren, Copplestone, Devon
Paul & Vicky Warren, Copplestone, Devon
Harold A., Mervyn J. & Horace G. Webber, Morchard Bishop, Devon
Maurice, Hilda, Brian & Sandra Wedlake, Crediton, Devon
The Wensley Family, formerly of Top Thatch Cottage, Morchard Bishop, Devon
C. J. Whicher, Woodgate House, Morchard Bishop, Devon
S. M. Wide, Worthing, West Sussex
Joyce M. Williams, Exeter, Devon
Brian, Wendy & Jack Wilshaw, Morchard Bishop, Devon
Mrs Katherine Xulu, Morchard Bishop, Devon
M. F. Yendell, Barton House, Morchard Bishop, Devon
Mr F. P. Yendell, Morchard Bishop, Devon
W. E. Yendell, Morchard Bishop, Devon

THE BOOK OF MORCHARD BISHOP

Also available in the Community History Series:

Widecombe-in-the-Moor Stephen Woods
Lanner – A Cornish Mining Parish Sharron Schwartz and Roger Parker
The Book of Cornwood and Lutton, Photographs and Reminiscences compiled by the People of the Parish
Postbridge –The Heart of Dartmoor Reg Bellamy
The Book of Bampton Caroline Seward
The Ellacombe Book Sydney R. Langmead
The Book of Lamerton, A Photographic History
The Book of Loddiswell, Heart of the South Hams The Loddiswell Parish History Group
The Book of Manaton
The Book of Meavy
The Book of North Newton J.C. Robins and K.C. Robins
The Book of Plymtree, The Parish and Its People, compiled and edited by Tony Eames
The Book of Porlock Dennis Corner
The Book of Stithians, The Changing Face of a Cornish Parish Stithians Parish History Group
The Book of Torbay, A Century of Celebration Frank Pearce
The Book of Trusham Alice Cameron
The Book of Werrington Joan Rendell MBE
Widecombe-in-the-Moor Revisited Stephen Woods
Woodbury, The Twentieth Century Revisited, compiled by Roger Stokes

Further information:
If you would like to find out more about having your parish featured in this series, please write to The Editor, Community History Series, Halsgrove House, Lower Moor Way, Tiverton Business Park, Tiverton, Devon, EX16 6SS, tel: 01884 243242 or visit us at http://www.halsgrove.com
If you are interested in a particular photograph in this volume, it may be possible to supply you with a copy of the image.